Let Your Heart Go Free

An Emancipation of the Soul

JEREMY AUSTILL

To Him; it's all worship.

To Michelle, who believes deeply with me.

To Bubby and Beetle, this is your inheritance.

To Mom, who kept me in His house.

To Dad, wish you could have seen this.

To the TYM Family, this was for your hearts first.

CONTENTS

FOREWORD

was drawn to him. Years ago, as he stood in a room of more than a thousand loud, worshiping young people who filled the auditorium of The Ramp, I noticed him. After leading this ministry of awakening for several years and seeing thousands of young men and women walk through its doors, I began to recognize something. True seekers always stand out in the crowd. You can spot them because they're different—in the most wonderful kind of way.

The eyes of true seekers are intensely looking for something. They are searching for Someone they have caught only a glimpse of. Their faces are aglow from standing in His presence. They are fueled by a passionate hunger for more of God. They are not seeker-sensitive. They don't care what it takes or how long it takes—they just want to find God. They don't have all the answers, and they like it that way.

True seekers ask questions, a lot of questions, because they are never satisfied with the status quo. Instead, they are compelled by the Voice that whispers, "There's more," and they will follow that Voice wherever He leads, even through the deepest caverns of the heart.

Yes, that is why he stood out among the many, and that is why I still respect him today. Jeremy Austill is a true seeker.

Out of Jeremy's own searching heart this book was written. As you walk with him through these pages, you will feel as though you are talking to a friend who "gets you," someone who is speaking directly to the questions you didn't even know you had.

You will be challenged to confront wrong mindsets with which you have become very comfortable. These mindsets express themselves in your everyday life. They affect your relationships and most especially your walk with God. They are often disguised in religious traditions that seem good and normal, but they are robbing you of your true identity and the abundant life our Father has provided.

These mindsets do not form overnight. They slowly weave their way into your thinking until what should be easy and light becomes heavy and burdensome. It happens so subtly you are often not even aware you have become entangled in a web of deception until you are confronted with a word of truth. That is why Paul expressed his concerns to the Corinthian church, "But I fear that somehow your pure and undivided devotion to Christ will be corrupted, just as Eve was deceived by the cunning ways of the serpent" (2 Corinthians 11:3).

These deceptive mindsets will complicate the simplicity and purity of your Father's plan for relational intimacy with Him. However, a true revelation of your Father's love for you will shatter the lies of the enemy and destroy the fear of never being able to measure up to what you thought He required.

Jesus did not die on the cross for you to live your life spiritually frustrated and exhausted, constantly trying to gain the acceptance of God and man. His death and resurrection opened wide the door to His heart, and like children we run in to discover the vastness of His love and the beauty of His Kingdom.

I believe you are holding this book in your hands because your own searching heart has caused you to reach out for the "more of God." With the wisdom of an experienced guide and the familiarity of a brother, Jeremy Austill will lead you through the door and walk you into unknown places of the heart. But with this invitation comes a promise, "Seek, and you will find."

There is one thing I have learned about God—He never disappoints a true seeker.

—Karen Wheaton
Singer, Worship Leader, Minister, The Ramp, Hamilton, Alabama

INTRODUCTION

According to my mother, I have been a born-again Christian since I was five years old. I don't really have a memory of the specific moment I surrendered myself over to the life of Christ. At the age of fifteen I sensed an intense call to serve the Lord through the activity of preaching His gospel. I preached my first sermon when I was seventeen, and by the time I was twenty years old preaching was my vocation, in addition to leading people and ministry in the body of Christ. For the duration of that time and until recent years, I strove to be a better person. I have strained to be a "better Christian." I have attended conferences, read books, listened to audios of great leaders—all with the goal of becoming a better version of me. Immersing myself fully into a life of self-perfection, I sought out every guru and model that could possibly empower me to become what I hoped I was capable of becoming. You likely picked up this book with similar intentions. We have a perpetual craving to be better. We have access to all of our personal inadequacies. We are all too familiar with our places of weakness and the true motives of our heart. We are intimately acquainted with every flaw and frailty. Therefore, we expend our finances, our time and energy trying to modify said imperfections.

If only we can diminish this habit...

Maybe if we cultivate a new system of operating...

Possibly, if we establish some rigidity to our daily schedule, we can will ourselves to a greater dimension of efficiency, morality, and success.

If we can just make ourselves better, we will be happy, fulfilled, and at peace as our head rests upon the pillow at night. On the surface this sounds like a noble endeavor, but what if it isn't? What if that longing and

9

searching is derived not from a place of healthy personal development but from a region of the soul that has a lack of revelation of the beauty and splendor of our God instead?

The majority of the leadership and Christian life books I have read are highly focused on self. They are structured on the premise that if I can get my act together sufficiently, I will be of greater use to society, attain higher degrees of success, and find satisfaction in my body of work. The problem with a self-help curriculum is that there is an overreliance on self to attain that which can only truly be imparted via the Divine One. What if the key to the door of true inward freedom and peace is not found in my ability to self-discipline and refine my skills? What if there is a "key of David" that opens doors no man can close and closes doors no man can open? What if my ever-present frustration is actually being fed and watered by my straining? What if my real problem is that I am constantly trying to be better? In the process, my eyes remain fixed on the mirror. I look at the mirror, observing every blemish and concocting strategies to eradicate them. Yet my eyes are still on me, in the mirror.

> ## What if there is a "key of David" that opens doors no man can close and closes doors no man can open?

What happens when we cease our efforts to be a better person and instead increase our knowledge of a divine Father? I will tell you quite simply what happens—our eyes get redirected from an earth-ravaged being to an eternal entity. We no longer seek contentment and satisfaction in the faulty systems of a fading world. We find, in a heavenly Father, all that we have ever needed and hoped for. We shift from a pursuit of happiness to an impartation of joy. We transition from hoping to be accepted among our peers to being loved immeasurably. We maneuver from the fickle approval of people to the unwavering validation of a time-tested Redeemer. My hope, as you read the coming pages, is that your heart will be freed from the confinements of shame; your mind will be redeemed from the processes of this world and your soul will finally be synced with the Spirit of God the way Jesus intended when He gasped His last breath on the cross and resumed His breathing in the tomb. You were born again to be free to the full. It is for freedom that He set you free!

Throughout this book there will be moments without concrete answers. There will be questions posed. There will be opportunities to enter new gates of understanding. If all the answers are placed blatantly before us, then the necessity of seeking ceases. Therefore, our relationship with the divine One is not as much about answers as it is seeking, pursuing, and discovering. If we are not careful in our pursuit of clarity and answers, we will miss Jesus who has been, is, and will always be *the* Answer. If we always allow others to spoon feed us with pat, cliché answers, we will live with the unsatisfactory gnawing of "that's not enough."

> ## Answers can be more dangerous than ignorance if they cause us to cease our exploration.

Answers can be more dangerous than ignorance if they cause us to cease our exploration. If answers cause us to set up camp, we have missed the greater purpose of following Jesus—a continual following that has no destination. I admit it. I don't have all of the answers. To hack away at my laptop with the arrogance that I can figure out your life is an affront to the loving God who uniquely designed you and is far more familiar with your circumstances than I. I am a fellow follower of Jesus who is asking the same questions you are. Yet I do so with the understanding that answers and convenient solutions fail to quench the thirst in my soul. Each life scenario and crossroad of questioning is an invitation to come a little closer and deeper into the One. Answers are not notches in the belt waved high as an emblem that shows we have conquered. It is the design of the Spirit to usher us through new gates of understanding and new dimensions of intimacy with the One who loves us most. I do not presume this book will fill in every blank. Therefore, throughout this book there is a verse that will be subtly pervasive and relied upon heavily.

> But you have received the Holy Spirit, and he lives within you, so you don't need anyone to teach you what is true. For the Spirit teaches you everything you need to know, and what he teaches is true—it is not a lie. So just as he has taught you, remain in fellowship with Christ (1 John 2:27).

You have been equipped with the greatest Teacher in the universe. My prayer is that as I talk to you through this ink on paper, Holy Spirit will speak deeply and pen the ways of His kingdom in your soul.

PROLOGUE:
JOURNEY MATTERS

For a moment, consider your favorite fictional book. You could take me to the last chapter of the book and have me read through the content. In those closing pages I would receive much pertinent information. I would likely discover the identity of the protagonist, learn the names of several central characters, and work through the conclusion of the book's ultimate conflict. From those fifteen to twenty pages I could surmise a few details in the plot through deductive reasoning and have a general idea of what took place over the preceding 300 pages. Yet all the information I gather by reading the last chapter would mean little to me emotionally. It would be a collection of facts, more information for the lifelong database that is the mind. But I would not necessarily be moved or affected by it. I wouldn't feel anything. The information would be hollow, lacking in weight and substance because of the absence of context. Having information is nice, but it is the journey to get that information that gives it weight in our lives. It is the journeying with the narrative that makes the information important on a deep enough level to affect one's existence. Information rarely changes a person. It is the journey to that information that changes one's life.

Unfortunately, the version of faith most often employed by modern believers is heavy on information and low on journey. We have answers, memorized Scriptures, quaint quips, which we forget are not actually derived from the Bible, and we have a general overview of what we are supposed to think and believe. We have a fill-in-the-blank rendition of religion that never quite satisfies on the level we know it ought. Why is that? We devalue process in exchange for hurrying up to the end. We are so obsessed with the punch line that once we get there, it feels empty. Information is hollow and lacking in resonance unless we live within in it, asking difficult questions, being content with what we deem are insufficient answers.

One of the great frailties of the American education system is its foundation. The intellectual development of a young person is deeply intertwined with the ability to give the right answer on the test. Early on, a child learns the way to gain affirmation and validation is to perform well on the test. Good grades are connected to right answers and the compilation of enough correct answers over an educational career allows one to graduate. Intimate understanding is minimized in favor of: "Is this going to be on the test?" I can't say I know a better way for our educational system to function. However, I can say this overt emphasis on results through answers becomes thoroughly implanted in our thinking and is not confined to our schooling. This is especially true in the life of faith.

Our ideas of discipleship gravitate toward learning what we are supposed to think, reading a couple of books, and becoming acquainted with the appropriate Scripture for the situation. Jesus is a person who wants to know and be known. Genuine, meaningful relationship cannot be rushed. I can know the high school you attended, the job you have, the names of your kids, and the type of automobile you drive, but none of these tidbits indicate that I actually know you. I can glean those facts by looking at your social media profile.

> ## Jesus is a person who wants to know and be known.

There is something beautiful in a secure, tenured relationship. A glance or a specific phrase has the power to pull the two people together and draw them into a distant, shared memory. I can make a statement in the presence of many, and my wife standing beside me hears it much differently than anyone else because we have over twenty years of context behind everything we say. I can tell a story from some past experience and others laugh at the circumstances within my tale. She not only laughs with joy, but also has a tinge of sorrow for that time gone by and a sense of fulfillment for the circumstances of our life at the time of the story. Information transcends facts and answers when combined with journey.

I say all of the above so you are aware that the coming pages are a journey for me and the Lord. This is not a textbook of material, but day-by-day revelation of my faith experience, and I have written it as such. I have felt led of the Lord to use a template to assist me in relaying my pilgrimage from a bound Christian (yes, a bound Christian) to a man whose heart is growing increasingly free. Throughout the duration of this book, John 1:1-13 will be the highway down which we will progress. I will go ahead and tell you, the crescendo is found in verse twelve.

> But to all who believed and accepted him, he gave the
> right to become children of God (John 1:12).

If you want, you can skip to the last couple of chapters and get the basic information in this book, but I promise the journey will give it more weight. Just like your relationship with Jesus, you will get there when you get there. Why rush off to the next answer? Enjoy the walk. You may see something even better on the way than what you find at the end of the road.

CHAPTER 1: BE

I am going to begin with a rebuttal to the coming thoughts. Depending on your preferred Bible translation, you may have this verse etched in your memory with particular phrasing. I grew up primarily with the King James Version so in my young world it sounded like this:

> But be ye doers of the word, and not hearers only, deceiving your own selves (James 1:22, KJV).

In our Americanized Western society we place a high priority on being people of action. We value and hold in esteem those who "get the job done" and are "about their Father's business." Contemplation, meditation, solitude, and reflection are, to a degree, intimidating concepts, often addressed with caution because those words are often attached to Eastern philosophies. *Doing* is more tangible. It yields more easily measured results. It is within our control. It is completely understandable that James 1:22 would be a lynchpin verse for a Western believer. I love the verse. I too want to be counted among those noted as doers of the word. However, notice there is an important word, which precedes doers; the word is *be*. One must sufficiently *be* before they will ever be compelled to consistently *do*. This is where we begin our journey.

> *"If you focus on your rights, you get rebellion; if you focus on your responsibility, you get revival."*
> —Anonymous

I was sitting in a hot metal building that served a dual purpose as a gymnasium for youth camp activities during the day and a sanctuary for God encounters at night. I was probably wearing something really trendy like a silk button-up shirt. I am certain the silk button-up shirt was saturated with sweat as the building did not have air conditioning and we were there on a hot June evening. That quote rang out from the evangelist's mouth, into the microphone, through the sound system, and settled into my soul. I have heard countless sermons and innumerable quotes through the years. Yet somehow, this declarative statement was seared into my memory and resurfaced vividly in recent years. It sounds good. It rolls off the tongue with ease. It is the kind of statement that compels you to nod in agreement. It pulls a "yes" from your lips. It conjures thoughts of the entitled and their soon-coming demise. It feels right and it sounds right. It is right, isn't it?

Could it be we have allowed many worldly thought processes to maintain residence in our thinking, despite our citizenship in a different realm?

What if I said there was a way which seemed right to a man but the end thereof was death (Proverbs 14:12)? I understand Solomon was likely talking about the fool, the deceiver, the liar, or the blatant sinner. However, it seems that very often as believers we are prone to embrace earthbound concepts that sound appealing and correct upon first hearing. Could it be we have allowed many worldly thought processes to maintain residence in our thinking, despite our citizenship in a different realm? Is it possible we have harbored quotes like the one above and, in so doing, have cornered ourselves in a room full of shame, despair, intimidation, stress, and pain? The quote sounds like a solid truth. I am not saying it's completely inaccurate. I am certain that the heart of the man who delivered it was pure and sincere. Yet for years I have meditated on my responsibility, delegitimized the notion that I have rights, and as a result have been incredibly conflicted internally. What would happen if our focus shifted?

Let's review:

JEREMY AUSTILL

"If you focus on your rights, you get rebellion; if you focus on your responsibility, you get revival."
—Anonymous

But to all who believed him and accepted him, he gave the right to become children of God (John 1:12).

We will return to this verse later in the book, but I wanted to juxtapose it with the quote in question. It seems John, the disciple whom Jesus loved, upon introducing Jesus clearly as divine, saw fit to emphasize the fact that believers (and accepters) are afforded rights. God offers us sonship. We can be sons and daughters of God. We can be part of His family.

I understand the struggle with the tension between rights and responsibilities. We live in a human society that is conflicted on its stance concerning entitlement versus contribution. In our American democratic government, there is much discourse centered on finding the balance between the rights and responsibilities of our citizenry. If you listen closely to the suited-up, so-called unbiased media you will notice much of their loud discussion repeatedly gravitates toward what a citizen is entitled to, and how much they are required to contribute to the whole. Personally, I have serious reservations about supernaturally infused people becoming so overtly fixed on a humanly devised governmental structure. Simply stated, I am not interested in becoming distracted by politics. American politics has devolved into another version of entertainment. People adhere political party stickers on their cars in the same fashion that they wear the jersey of their favorite team—with little regard for the spiritual hopelessness it represents. I wonder if we have become falsely dependent upon a carnal structure to accomplish victory in a battle that requires spiritual weaponry. But I digress.

I want to return to the earlier quote and make it clear that I do not wholeheartedly disagree with its content or intent. I do struggle with where it positions me as it relates to my Father though. The quote was a noble call to action, a call to selflessness. However, it also subtly resonates with a tinge of guilt. In the church, we have become proficient at relating the responsibility of the believer to contribute through lectures, print, and preaching from pulpits. We have asked everyone to bring something to the table for the benefit of the whole. We have encouraged, pled, begged, and possibly used versions of guilt and bribery for the purpose of compelling people to be involved.

Involved—what an interesting word. Involved with what? Are we genuinely asking people to step into the arena of God's kingdom or have we unintentionally (with sincere motives) shamed others and ourselves to activity on the hamster wheel of a busy organization, where favor is garnered through performance and adherence to the unwritten rules? Regarding motives, I would hate to inspect mine through the years as I cherry-picked Scripture to get the church commitment I desired, not so much for the betterment of people or the benefit of His kingdom but rather as a response to my own insecurity.

From the perspective of someone in a place of spiritual leadership, we get frustrated when the message of involvement is heard but not received to the point of action. After immense effort to compel people to assume more responsibility in the "spiritual" work-load, we find ourselves surrounded by decreased commitment, sporadic attendance, and diminished consistency. I wonder how effective it is to repeatedly tell people they need to *do* something. Maybe it is of greater value to call a people to *be* something. We are occasionally numb to it in ourselves (and clearly see it in others), but we all have some disconnect between knowing what to do and actually acting upon that knowledge.

Maybe it is the Generation X in me, but I am at the point in life and faith where I am exhausted with hearing what I need to do. I am willing to admit I may be in the minority here. I have a plethora of knowledge on what it is I need to do as a devout follower of Jesus. The database is extensive. After forty or so years of church life, a Bible college degree, and roughly two decades of preaching, I have a ridiculous amount of information on how I am to conduct myself in order to be perceived as an adequate Christian. Yet, it often feels empty. It feels like ritual. It feels like routine and practice.

I know what to do. You probably have a pretty sound idea on what to do yourself. The problem is that doing, alone, can create malfunctions. Any *doing* not derived from *being* is hard labor, which produces fatigue and frustration. I wonder if you have felt the exhaustion in your soul of doing without a legitimate source. I am not speaking of physical fatigue but of the draining of your thinking, emotions, and will. It seems that much of our effort in "churchdom" is rooted in this—that more people would become hooked on our church and ministry. Obviously, this is not the stated goal. We proclaim that it's all about Jesus; but even for the spiritual leader, I wonder how much of our labor is motivated from the source of being and how much is from the obligation of this work having to be done. How "right" it feels to man to be extremely devoted to a church, a ministry, the mission? It feels very right. But could it be that for many of us, it has become a way that is leading us to death instead of life? This path, which appears to be so noble on the surface, leads to heartache and a dearth of fulfillment. We do, we contribute, we handle our responsibility…on and on and on we go. Then we notice that we are becoming increasingly numb, disinterested, disappointed, ragged, and frustrated. It takes a long time, but there we are.

> ## Any *doing* not derived from *being* is hard labor, which produces fatigue and frustration.

I fear we have a large percentage of people in the body of Christ who know how to do church but have no idea how to *be* in Christ. Is it possible that if we set our eyes on Jesus and became more involved in His presence, more explorative of His Word, more leaned into his heart, all of the serving, working, doing, and involvement would carry more substantial meaning and feel less cumbersome? I wonder if we have put the proverbial cart before the horse. We try to compel people closer to God by signing them up for a list of responsibilities. We try to wedge people into a relationship with the Lord by engaging them in activity. It is an age-old admonition, which rolls off the tongue easily but seems more difficult to usher into reality. Our labor, our responsibility, our involvement should flow out of our connection to Jesus and not the other way around. We have heard that we should take responsibility, do something, show up, punch the clock, and do work often enough. Maybe we need to pause and reflect—not so much on what we need to do but more on what He has done. Let's do that for the next few chapters.

CHAPTER 2: DREAM

Does God have dreams for you?

If so, what does He dream?

I remember the first series I preached as a youth pastor. It was centered on a phrase common to our society: "Dream Big." Is there a concept more celebrated in Americana than living a life with big dreams? I'm sure there is, but certainly this one is among those found at the top of the list. To this day I am an advocate for living with a high level of belief, seeing life through the lens of possibility, and being a person with hope flowing through your veins. If we are indeed loved beyond comprehension by God, it only seems reasonable to believe He has dreams for our lives. It may prove beneficial to explore the nature of God's dreams over us, His beloved.

John gives us a unique glimpse of Jesus and, as a result, a beautiful perspective on how we fit into the Jesus narrative. This is the same John who was a revelator on Patmos, embracing Mary at the foot of the cross, reclined against Jesus at the Last Supper, and standing in awe on the Mount of Transfiguration. Maybe more than any other man who penned the story of Jesus, John saw Him and grasped the totality of His divinity and the nature of His supernatural kingdom. It would be wise, in our pause, to survey his introduction of Jesus.

In order to sufficiently perceive the hopes of heaven for our earthly existence and its eternal ramifications, we must turn our attention to the beginning of all things. And that is exactly where John initiates his rendition of the gospel.

> In the beginning the Word already existed. The Word
> was with God, and the Word was God. He existed in the
> beginning with God. God created everything through him,
> and nothing was created except through him (John 1:1-3).

Before we are specifically introduced to the Son of God in the flesh
through the Gospels, we discover Him as being intrinsically active in
the inception of all things. He was so present at creation that everything
devised in the imagination of God was funneled through God the Son. It
was all touched by Him and exposed to Him, humanity included. Bear
with me for a few moments as we wade into some theological waters.
There is a principle in biblical interpretation called the Law of First
Mention. This principle requires one to go to the portion of Scriptures
where a doctrine or process of thought is mentioned for the first time
and study the first occurrence in order to get inherent, implied meaning
of that doctrine or thought process. Upon inspecting the first mention,
we gain understanding of God's original intent and create a foundation
for perceiving the doctrine or thought process throughout the rest of the
Bible. John 1 hearkens us back to Genesis, which is the ultimate First
Mention book of the Bible. In the creation account of man, it is possible
we have been given some deeply valuable clues about how God dreams
over us as a people and individuals. I want us to turn our attention to
three specific details about the construction of man.

> Then the Lord God formed the man from the dust of the
> ground. He breathed the breath of life into the man's nostrils,
> and the man became a living person (Genesis 2:7).

It would be overly simplistic to view this verse strictly through the
scientific demand for oxygen. Yes, God was creating within the human
body the system of breathing, giving permission to vital organs to
operate at peak performance. However, there is a greater truth to be
found in this verse beyond God giving man the ability to use the air
around him to sustain his bodily functions. The verse states plainly, "He
breathed." God breathed. The divine, supernatural, heavenly, spiritual
breath of God was released from His person and used as a catalyst for

life in man. If God were merely giving man lung capacity, He could have drawn from the winds of the earth. He could have pulled from the surrounding oxygen. Instead, God took of His own life and with it invigorated man. The implication is that God's creation of man was enlivened with the understanding that man functions at optimal capacity with the unceasing flow of the breath of God.

> ## What if He was saying that without His unceasing flow in, through, and out of us, we cannot survive the life of faith?

I have a rudimentary understanding of human biology. I was a pretty bad science student, but I sat in enough classes to glean this little nugget: Deprived of oxygen, the human body loses its ability to live. Organs die, appendages shrink, and damage is done. As I said, rudimentary. What if in Genesis 2:7 the Lord was conveying a prophetic message? What if He was saying that without His unceasing flow in, through, and out of us, we cannot survive the life of faith? We will address this thought more specifically at a later time. For the time being, allow yourself to identify that in this first mention of mankind the very breath of God was released into our being. We are not speaking about oxygen but a supernatural flow, a spiritual vitality, a refreshing breeze that can be as constant as oxygen. What else can we observe in the creation of man?

> Then the Lord God planted a garden in Eden in the east,
> and there he placed the man he had made (Genesis 2:8).

Not only did God construct man from the dust of the earth and breathe into his nostrils, He also established him in a place of residence. None of us can speak with certainty of the aesthetics of the garden. We can imagine the lush vegetation, the free roaming animals, the rich soil, the soft grass, and the vividly blue skies. Yet all we can do is create images in the mind. The text does offer us a clue to the nature of living within Eden. The Hebrew translation of the word *Eden* is best summed up with the words *delight* and *pleasure*. We may not know the appearance of

Eden, but we can surmise the living conditions. In choosing a home for man, God created a space called delight and pleasure. The first place God established man to live in was filled with delight and pleasure.

For some, our theology gives us pause here. We struggle with the idea that the Lord is concerned with our delight and pleasure. God did not construct a spot that was rigid, harsh, and demanding as a place of habitation for mankind. Is it possible that through the lens of First Mention we can deduce that God intended us to experience a life of relief, joy, pleasure, delight, and wonder? Not only is it possible, I believe it is a truth. We will revisit this in a moment; but before doing so, let's take a look at one more portion of the first communication about man and his relationship to God.

> When the cool evening breezes were blowing, the man
> and his wife heard the Lord God walking about in the
> garden (Genesis 3:8a).

Let me first establish that this verse is on the heels of Adam and Eve devouring the forbidden fruit. We will spend a little time examining this moment of sin in the coming pages. However, the implied thought here is the presumably common practice of God visiting the garden and walking throughout it. If you have been in church many times you have likely heard a sermon, or at least a reference, to walking with God in the cool of the day. Apparently, the sound of God's arrival was familiar to Adam and Eve because they recognized it. They heard Him. How did they know it was Him? It is relatively safe to assume this was not a one-time occurrence but probably a consistent practice. God, descending from His throne to walk alongside and engage personally with His precious creation! God, the most profound Being of all, vast beyond comprehension, strong beyond imagination, friend of His beloved man.

Within these opening pages of Scripture, there was the charge from heaven for man to live in dominion over earth and all it held. Adam was assigned the responsibility of naming the living creatures. Yes, Adam and Eve had some responsibilities; but in man's origin, there is no language communicating a weighty, cumbersome existence. There is no indication the labor was exhausting, nor was fatigue pervasive. Man was at work in creation, but man was at peace. Man had an assignment but it was not laced with stress, frustration, and discontent. Man and woman were active on God's behalf, but in the midst of the doing was great delight and pleasure.

What is God's dream for you?
Himself.

This may be slightly challenging for some who hold intensely to conventional societal thinking; but once embraced, a door is opened that unveils beautiful mysteries and releases the adornments of true kingdom living.

God's dream, His plan, His intent for you has very little to do with your calling, your ministry, your job, your success, your status, your accomplishments, your effectiveness, your influence, or your results. God's dream for you is that you would breathe in the freshness of His Spirit, allow Him to course through your being and be released into the world around you. God's dream for you is an intimate intertwining of you and His Spirit to the degree that you experience the consistent and persistent flow of His life in, through, and from your soul. He has eternally imagined connectivity between you and Him—a "with-ness" that eliminates the gaps of time between encounters. He dreams not of meeting you on Sunday but of flowing with abundant life through the proverbial veins of your soul every day. God's dream for you is that your life is drenched with pleasure and delight, a pleasure and delight marked by friendship with Him and rooted in His love for you.

What is God's dream for you?

Himself.

Take a moment and meditate on this idea.

Allow the idea of His dream to roll around in your soul.

LET YOUR HEART GO FREE

As simple and obvious as it may sound, we tend to add unnecessary weights to the dream that press against us and wear us to the core.

If we call Him a good Father, this is the only acceptable dream He can have for our lives. There is nothing in this galaxy or 10,000 galaxies that compares to His splendor. There is nothing in the heavens above or the earth below capable of withstanding the majesty of His stature. There is no entity known or unknown as immeasurable in desirable attributes. His love is high, long, wide, and deep. His knowledge is beyond our capacity. His ways defy our reasoning. His mercy is unquenchable. His peace challenges our understanding. His joy causes our descriptive words to fail in communicating the fullness of His glory.

I am a dad. I would like to think I am a good dad, although I assume time will ultimately tell the tale. In my finite fatherhood, I carry in my heart great hopes and dreams for the little boy and girl sleeping down the hall. I crave the best for them both. Comparing my temporal fatherly desires to our eternal Father, it only seems fitting He would have hopes and dreams for us of the highest quality. Simply stated, Yahweh can dream no bigger for me than Himself. The best, wildest, most incredible dream He can imagine is Himself. He would be less than a father to dream something substandard to Himself.

Deeply consider this reality! God's dream for you is not about the work you do for Him; it is more so the measure of Him you take on and allow to saturate your life. I understand that in this moment the achiever, the accomplisher, the doer of the Word is likely cringing and preparing a barrage of counterarguments. It would be easy to cherry-pick from the Bible and say, "What about this? What about that?"

I know this portion of me certainly struggles with the notion that God is content with me and doesn't limit His perception of me to what I produce for Him. It is the American in me. It is the earner in me that cries out, "You get what you deserve! You earn your keep! You must prove yourself!" That portion of who I am contends in a moment like this. You can evaluate the tension and continue assuming it is reasonable thinking and good theology because it fits our cultural narrative, or you can settle into the truth that God is more interested in you than the harvest you yield. Yes we have responsibility. Yes we have a mission. Yes we have a Great Commission. But remember, *doing* that is not derived from *being* is hard labor that births exhaustion and frustration. Do I want you to have a good job, tremendous success, a great ministry, and remarkable productivity? Absolutely! I am pausing right now to pray those things for you as you read.

> In the designs of God, He built us with a mechanism of satisfaction, which is only legitimately triggered by a firm connection to Him.

In the designs of God, He built us with a mechanism of satisfaction, which is only legitimately triggered by a firm connection to Him. As humans we have a mental hurdle with this because when we create, it is for the purpose of productivity or usefulness or success or money. We create a machine to accomplish a job. We create a gadget to make life more convenient. We create a product that will enhance our business. God created us for companionship. He did not create us for productivity because He doesn't need us for the purpose of accomplishment. We are unnecessary to "get God's job done." His dream is for you to have Him—to the full. Everything else leaves us lacking.

Drink it in one more time.

God's dream for you is Him.

CHAPTER 3: PARADISE LOST

remember the moment vividly. I was in the first grade on the far edge of the playground out of earshot from our teachers or any other authority figures, surrounded by my friends. The region in western Tennessee where I grew up was notorious for substantial erosion issues. It is a place of fertile farmland, but the soil, so nutrient rich for crop growth, is also easily disturbed by rain and moving water. On the outer rim of the elementary school playground was a sloped area that consistently washed out when the rains came. The grass didn't grow and it looked like a miniature model of the Grand Canyon with ditches, recesses, and ruts carved deeply into the crusted soil. There among my six-year-old peers I found myself, stick in hand, digging in the dirt. On the surface this was a seemingly innocent scene. What I didn't realize was that I was sitting in the middle of a toxic situation.

One of my friends joined me in the act of digging in the dirt. Along with the boys from our class, my digging buddy and I were also encircled by a healthy population of girls. At first the occasional outburst of giggling girls was mere background noise to the task at hand. To this day I have no idea what we were trying to accomplish, but more and more frequently I noticed my friend was able to induce glee from the young ladies and affirmation from the guys. As I observed more closely, my ears picked up on a familiar compilation of syllables. I had attended enough church to know this particular combination of sounds coming from someone's mouth was not good; as a matter of fact, as far as I was concerned, it was sinful. But I was mesmerized by my "friend's" sway over the crowd with the use of those words—cuss words. Here I am digging

31

just as diligently and with as much effectiveness as my buddy, but all the attention centered on his mouth. They all seemed to hang on every quiver of his lip, longingly anticipating his next entertaining expletive.

My first grade logic knew those words out of my mouth would be a violation of conscience, but maybe I could euphemism my way into the admiration of my classmates. I reached for the closest, not quite sinful, word I could find that closely resembled its vulgar counterpart. I didn't quite cuss, but I hoped I got close enough to the real thing to garner attention. Instead, I was met with a reprimand by my earth-digging compatriot. He chastised me for not actually saying a cuss word and then he threatened to excommunicate me from the dirt quarry if I did not fully invest in the present vernacular. After a couple more attempts at appeasement via euphemism it became clear I had a choice to make: Cuss or leave!

I cussed.

I said the "S" word.

For the first time in my life I blatantly and consciously chose to defy my conscience and conviction. I knew I had offended God. From there I joined the rest of humanity on the slippery slope.

In the name of self-awareness, most of us look at our lives, not the external activity but the internal dialogue, and find that we struggle to simply breathe God in and out. We can identify substantial spaces in our lives that lack pleasure and delight. We live in a fallen world. We live in a defiled world, corrupt and now established upon faulty systems. How am I supposed to focus on breathing God and walk in legitimate pleasure and delight within a world diametrically opposed to the garden life? Sin entered. Sin eroded everything. My experience was a first-grade account. You have your own version of my "digging with a stick" story. You also have some familiarity with the story of the ages.

> The Lord God made all sorts of trees grow up from the
> ground—trees that were beautiful and that produced
> delicious fruit. In the middle of the garden he placed the

tree of life and the tree of the knowledge of good and evil (Genesis 2:9).

But the Lord God warned him, "You may freely eat the fruit of every tree in the garden—except the tree of the knowledge of good and evil. If you eat its fruit, you are sure to die" (Genesis 2:16-17).

The serpent was the shrewdest of all the wild animals the Lord God had made. One day he asked the woman, "Did God really say you must not eat the fruit from any of the trees in the garden?" (Genesis 3:1).

"You won't die!" the serpent replied to the woman. "God knows that your eyes will be opened as soon as you eat it, and you will be like God, knowing both good and evil" (Genesis 3:4-5).

Before we explore the layers of this conversation between Eve and the serpent, can I offer a brief aside, an observation that fascinates me about the account of Eve, a serpent, a tree, and devoured fruit? We find Eve, a woman, having a conversation with a snake, yet nothing in the text indicates she was fearful, anxious, stressed, or under duress. It is a little bit funny when you consider how this might play out in your backyard. A woman talking to a snake and she is not afraid. Let's take this a step further. Eve, a human, was having a conversation, not with a mere snake but with Lucifer himself. A human was dialoguing with the personification of evil, yet she was not quaking, shaking, or afraid. Of course, we know she made a terrible decision based upon the enticement of the snake; but don't lose sight of the fact that prior to her fall into sin, the concept of fear, worry, angst, and stress was absolutely foreign to her. Why? Because she had been established by God in delight and pleasure. We were not created to know or live in fear. You weren't born for fear or stress or anxiety. You were created fully capable of looking evil in the eye and being blanketed by peace. You were wired for something better than the strained existence that has become so familiar to us that it seems natural and acceptable. I know we live in a fallen world that has corrupted the dream of heaven…but God.

An entire book can be written, and many probably have, about the nature of the serpent's conversation with the woman. It appears, upon closer inspection, that the initial invitations of the fallen Lucifer to the woman are still being whispered in the ears of her offspring to this day. The serpent posed a question that still settles into the core of fallen man generations upon generations later.

Did God really say…?

For the follower of Jesus this may sound like a preposterous question with a slam-dunk response: "Of course God said! It is written in His Word! His Word is infallible! All Scripture is God-breathed and useful. God said it, I believe it, and that settles it!" Questions are funny. Sometimes there is the surface question, but underneath there is a labyrinth of subtext. At times a simple question is asked, but by listening closer subtle innuendos are detected. Satan was asking a heavier question than one focused upon the recitation of God's command. He was digging into the core of Eve. He was probing for fissures. He was looking for a crack in the door. He needed an opening into which his slithering tail could be placed. Eve gave her trained response. She gave her years of Sunday school answer: "God said we can't eat from that tree right there." She gave the correct answer, but clearly there was a breach in her soul.

God commanded, but is He really worthy of my trust?

God said, but based upon this new information is His statement still relevant?

God directed, but He created me and placed me in pleasure so surely He would not withhold something good from me.

God spoke, but my logic and reason says something a little different.

I know what God said, but it doesn't make sense in light of what I am seeing right in front of me.

Yes, He spoke, but His expectations seem so odd and out of touch with my present experience.

How clever and strategic the serpent must have been. How clever and strategic the serpent remains today. The subtle whisper, challenging the words of God, beckoning us to look around and view the absurdity of God's expectation. Here I am. In a moment, I can hear the echo of God's command, but this present enticement is more real than the echo. Did God really say? Does God really love me? Does this really matter to God? The plan of the fallen angel was so cliché: "Why don't you go ahead and doubt?" And the next layer of dialogue was equally cunning: "You won't die!" You can hear our thoughts in these words.

God said, but surely this won't end in my ruin.

God spoke, but this one time won't derail me.

His Word states, but no real pain will come.

However, reading this, you know the problem firsthand. We may not physically die, but something dies. Something goes cold. Something is drained to hollow. A deep grief nestles in our soul. We have a word from God. We have a declarative statement. How often does the distant sound of His voice lose to the allure of the immediate?

"Eve tried to navigate the temptation with her desires and passions at the helm. When we commit this error in judgment, we fall prey to the lie of 'just one.' We disconnect the moment of temptation from all other moments and dismiss our inner hesitations as overreactions because, we rationalize, this is only about one moment of splurging or one brief glance or one white lie or one...Stifling any concerns of bigger-picture consequences, we take a bite. The sweetness that passes our lips quickly turns rancid as we begin to taste the cold, metallic hook in our hearts. Pleasure can anesthetize us against that taste temporarily, but when it wears off (which is inevitable) the pain or shame we

35

LET YOUR HEART GO FREE

feel serves to reconnect us with reality."
—Alicia Britt Chole in her book, Anonymous[1]

The final nail in the temptation coffin is the appeal to believe that we are capable of adequately governing ourselves.

Oh, but the invitation is taken a little further by the enemy of our soul: "Your eyes will be opened. You will be like God." The final nail in the temptation coffin is the appeal to believe that we are capable of adequately governing ourselves. The person who picked this book up and is reading it is not the type of person to shout at the heavens "I can do a better job with my life than You can, God!" I know you aren't that person. Your enemy knows you aren't that person, but...

You will be like God, so make sure you work hard, store up treasures, and keep it all close by so you will never have the strain of depending upon Him. You can depend upon yourself.

You will be like God. You are intelligent and experienced. You can figure out the solution on your own, based upon what you have seen and learned up to this point.

You will be like God. God's answer to your situation may not line up with what your reason tells you, so just go ahead and figure it out own your own.

You will be like God, so you can make that decision based upon how things add up and come together. Do what makes sense, not what requires faith and trust and hope.

---

1. Alicia Britt Chole, PhD., *Anonymous: Jesus' Hidden Life...and Yours* (Nashville, TN: Thomas Nelson, 2011).

*You will be like God, so diminish the importance of
those portions of Scripture and expectations of the Lord
that create friction with your routine, your convenience,
and your preferences by buffeting your stance and your
current way of life with another portion of the Bible.*

*You will be like God, so you can downplay certain
attributes of God that are uncomfortable or don't
fit your agenda. You can elevate and proclaim the
attributes of God that better serve your purposes.*

As I type, I am fully aware that this invitation plays out differently dependent upon one's socio-economic status, region of residence, family history, and other variables. The sound is different for me as I deposit my middle-class paycheck and sit in the kitchen of my decent home in a quaint neighborhood. The nudge is different for me as I drive my two fully operational automobiles and hand my credit card over to the waiter at a relatively nice restaurant. The allure doesn't seem like such an inappropriate one as I sit on my leather couch watching my big screen TV with more channels than I could possibly watch. Here is what the whisper sounds like in my ear.

*You will be like God if you work hard enough. If you
work the system well enough, you can create for
yourself a place of pleasure and delight and will have
less use for God as the source of such niceties.*

*"God created man in his image and man returned the
compliment."*
—Blaise Pascal[2]

What was (and remains) the aim of the serpentine villain? Isn't it obvious? God dreams of us having Himself to a degree that we have

---

2. Blaise Pascal, *Pensees* (Paris: Garnier Frères, 1964).

unceasing connection, delight, pleasure, peace, joy, love, hope, patience, kindness, goodness, self-control, freedom, and so much more.

The vile rebel of heaven, who has proven his contempt toward God is of such great weight that it propelled him into the absurdity of mutiny, would like nothing more than to disrupt the dream of God. If he cannot depose God, maybe he can compel humanity to unwittingly evict themselves from the paradise of knowing God intimately. In the process he lances God where it hurts most by wounding His beloved. Whether it is the complete degradation that accompanies one who has made no step in God's direction or it is the suppression of the heart of the one who has said yes to Jesus, the hope of the enemy is to deny God and deny man. To deny God the joy of fellowship with His precious creation and to deny man the great pleasure found in his Father. Fortunately, the story has several acts—and the ending is glorious.

CHAPTER 4: SHAME

The woman was convinced. She saw that the tree was beautiful and its fruit looked delicious, and she wanted the wisdom it would give her. So she took some of the fruit and ate it. Then she gave some to her husband, who was with her, and he ate it, too. At that moment their eyes were opened, and they suddenly felt shame at their nakedness. So they sewed fig leaves together to cover themselves (Genesis 3:6-7).

The fruit has been eaten and disobedience has begun. Notice the emotional response of Adam and Eve upon the realization that they had sinned against God. They suddenly felt shame. We often attach shame to the word *embarrassment*, but the two are not really similar. Embarrassment pertains to circumstances. Shame goes much deeper. The best way to explain "shame" is to view it in comparison with "guilt." Guilt is the sense that I did something wrong. Shame is defined as the sense there is something wrong *with* me.

It is a common idea in the arena of psychology that shame is a central figure in many psychological disorders. Shame assaults the place of identity and is a root for low self-esteem and weakened self-image. It creates doubt and erodes confidence. Shame hinders intimacy, causes barriers to be entrenched within us, and plunges a person into inferiority complexes. Shame is often the driving force behind perfectionism. Shame is the root of many of the psychological and emotional struggles people endure.

What is the root of shame? Sin. What is the goal of sin based upon God's Word about sin as an entity crouching at the door (Genesis 4:7)?

Control. What better way to control than to distort the view a person has of one's self? If sin can tightly clench its fist around a person's self-worth, it is inevitable that God-defying actions will soon follow. Sin latches on to our soul and releases the toxin of shame. At the time of their act of defiance, shame was a legitimate emotion for Adam and Eve. The same is true in this present hour. When we sin, something is wrong with us. Prior to salvation, we should feel shame because something was intensely wrong with us. We had been separated from union with God and were defiled in every way imaginable. We were living in the throes of having been violated by sin and were active in the violation of ourselves. Something was wrong with us. We were dead. What an incredible strategy by our enemy—to make the prized jewel of creation feel unworthy, disgusting, weak, insecure, fearful, and unlovable. Sin wants us to be frustrated with, and disappointed in, ourselves; for if we are angry with ourselves, how can we adequately receive the love of God? How can we sufficiently offer love to God if we are such a mess? Shame and sin have a spiraling affect.

> Then the Lord God said, "Look, the human beings have become like us, knowing both good and evil. What if they reach out, take fruit from the tree of life, and eat it? Then they will live forever!" So the Lord God banished them from the Garden of Eden, and he sent Adam out to cultivate the ground from which he had been made (Genesis 3:22-23).

The result of Adam's and Eve's sin was a removal from Eden. It was a removal from a home in delight and pleasure. It is true that sin pushes us in the direction of a certain version of delight and pleasure—one highly self-centered, flesh-oriented, temporal, and both spiritually and physically detrimental to our souls. It is a counterfeit to the relief derived from being enveloped in unwavering love, contradictory peace, and non-circumstantial joy. An exchange is made in which we forfeit internal freedom for supposed external liberty. The problem is that in the generations-long human narrative, external pleasure cannot sufficiently numb internal strife. To look happy is fool's gold in comparison to legitimate joy. The aim of Satan in the garden is much the same today— that we evict ourselves from legitimate delight for a fleeting pleasure. Sin begets shame, and shame begets a cease of residence in God's pleasure and delight.

This eviction launches us into what the Declaration of Independence called the "pursuit of happiness." Blaise Pascal, in his writing *Pensees*, calls it "diversion." I cannot do justice to his treatise on the matter, but I would like to share some excerpts that will help explain the thought that the pursuit of happiness, although desirable, often serves as an inadequate remedy for the evicted soul.

> *"If man were (truly) happy, the less he were diverted*
> *the happier he would be, like the saints and God."*
> —Blaise Pascal,[3] *addition mine*

If a person were truly "happy," less would be more, because a man who is legitimately happy has found the most potent source of joy is in divine communion with his Father. While there are many wholesome pleasures in this life, none rise to the level of satisfaction that rich connection with Yahweh affords. It is natural to desire happiness and this desire is not one trampled on by God. I am in no way offering up the notion that one is not allowed hobbies or niceties. Yet the question must be asked, "Why are these things so important to me?"

> *"The only good thing for men therefore is to be*
> *diverted from thinking of what they are, either by some*
> *occupation which takes their mind off it, or by some*
> *novel and agreeable passion which keeps them busy,*
> *like gambling, hunting, some absorbing show, in short*
> *by what is called diversion."*
> —Blaise Pascal[4]

---

3. Ibid.

4. Ibid.

LET YOUR HEART GO FREE

Outside of a peace and joy offered in unbroken relationship with Holy Spirit, all things are insufficient and can serve as distractions, enabling one to avoid the deeper matters of the heart. If I can offer my attention to my favorite sports team, my favorite hobby, shopping, entertainment, work, or the purchase of luxuries, then I can anesthetize the parts of my soul that lack the delight and pleasure for which I am truly born.

> *"It is not that they really bring happiness, nor that anyone imagines that true bliss comes from possessing the money to be won at gaming or the hare that is hunted...What people want is not the easy peaceful life that allows us to think of our unhappy condition...but the agitation that takes our mind off it and diverts us."*
> —Blaise Pascal[5]

If we are not careful we will become experts in the art of distraction. When left to ponder ourselves and the health of our soul, we know there is anger or bitterness or disappointment or frustration or sorrow there. Rather than explore the root of those assaults to the soul, we expend ourselves in areas that help us not feel them. I understand some of this can be considered a broad generalization. It may not be applicable to you. I certainly do not want to convey the sense that every hobby or "diversion" is some deep soul cry for help. However, it is imperative that we search ourselves, by help of Holy Spirit, to discern if we are in the habit of covering up a lack of delight and pleasure with harmless activity.

It is heartbreaking that humanity as a whole and thus many individuals live outside the pleasure and delight of their wonderful Creator. Yet it seems equally tragic that so many who have whispered the "salvation prayer" at a tear-stained altar find themselves evicted from all He made available. While I understand shame may be a legitimate response to sin, it is disheartening how many people have been redeemed by the blood of Jesus, yet still carry heavy loads of shame. It seems, based upon

---

5. Ibid.

observation and personal experience, a very real possibility that my spirit can be revived from death to life and yet my soul still carry some of the toxins of my old life of sin. It grieves me, and I'm sure the Father too, to see His beloved, created once and then reborn into supernatural life, walking the earth—downtrodden, frustrated, heartbroken, and insecure.

- Do you feel the pangs of insecurity rise up when things don't quite go the way you had hoped?

- Do you sense the jealousy in your soul when someone else does well and you feel as if it was an indictment on all your inadequacies?

- Do you feel the pressure to be perfect because anything less exposes the "real you" to the world, and you don't feel they will love that version of you?

- Do you weigh every word in light of how you will be perceived? Are you fearful that people will not like you if you have one verbal misstep?

Do you live with that subtle pit in your gut because you feel like a fraud, a fake?

I could keep asking the questions. You probably could type out a few on your own. As a daddy, if my children were asking these questions, tears would roll bitterly down my face. Pondering the possibility of my young babies wrestling with such questions grieves me. To think that I have done so much to ensure they feel confident, secure, loved, and valued and their hearts bear such questioning would be gut-wrenching. I would not be an angry dad. I would be a dad who continually tried to sink the message into the hearts of my kids—the message that they are loved and have no need for shame. I would gather them to me and reaffirm who they really are. I would speak life and prophesy their true nature. Could it be that *the* Father is attempting to do just that in our life right now if we would only slow down, tune our ear, and listen? If we would cease with the game of diversion, is it possible He is whispering? Some of us look at sin and we see it as an obstruction to God's blessing on our productivity. We see sin as something that decreases our anointing, thus making us less effective. We view our sins too often in terms of how it will affect our effectiveness in the world around us. The real harm of sin is that it clouds our ability to properly see the Lord and ourselves.

> ## The real harm of sin is that it clouds our ability to properly see the Lord and ourselves.

How do we combat shame and eviction? With a right understanding of how we are perceived by God in light of His redemptive work!

I have the same clichéd account of so many fathers before me. It is amazing how smaller versions of yourself running through the house alter our perspective of God as a Father. It is beautiful to have our eyes of understanding illuminated about our heavenly Father. However, in the process we sometimes miss the revelation of our newfound existence as sons and daughters of eternal descent. We begin to grasp that He is a loving Father but we don't quite grasp that we are now the offspring of heaven. We are in this world but no longer confined to the trappings, misgivings, and temperaments of this world.

CHAPTER 5: DARK/LIGHT

As a male, I have come to accept that I have some innate deficiencies. One of the most prominent, which plays a recurring role in my married life, is my utter inability to find something when my wife asks me to look for it. More specifically, why does it seem that items in the refrigerator disappear when the door is opened? After years of study, I think we can put to bed the question of what happens to the refrigerator light when the door closes. Obviously, it turns off. But now a new question has crept to the surface: Where is the ketchup? It is unbelievably frustrating for me (and much more so for Michelle) when I swing open the stainless steel doors, anticipating an easy recon mission for some condiment or fresh produce, only to stare blankly for what seems unending minutes completely incapable of locating the desired object. I am looking in the refrigerator full of food and food type items and cannot hone my sight to get a glimpse of the one thing I really need in the moment.

I wonder if on some level, my poor search skills serve as an adequate analogy of how I have perceived sin through the years. I have opened the theological and doctrinal doors and I see all the thoughts and ideas that have been stored concerning sin. But it seems, for many years, that I stared blankly into my own soul, unable to locate the one thing I needed to understand most. All of the information I have is wonderful and helpful. However, the fully stocked repertoire of truth nuggets I had on the concept of sin fell terribly short in helping me overcome its grip in my life for a very long time.

- What is it we are missing?
- Why do I struggle to break from these well-worn patterns?

- If Jesus is as profound in His abilities as I believe Him to be, why do I still feel the vice grip of sin in certain areas of my life?

- Why can't I shake the tendencies I have that leave me ever disappointed in myself?

I don't intend to oversimplify, but sometimes the mysteries of God are not that mysterious. We are staring right at them. They have been there all along. Far too often we observe sin through the fruit plucked from the limb and pressed to the lips. We converge our thoughts and energy upon the action of disobedience. We perceive sin as something we do instead of accurately understanding its true form. It is easier to concentrate on self-discipline, will power, schedule changes, and elimination of temptation triggers than to ask the deeper questions: Why does Eve eat the fruit? Why did Adam follow suit? Why do I repeatedly do that? What causes me to respond that way? Be careful here. I am not necessarily talking about the dredging up of past scars and childhood dysfunction to pinpoint our present behavior. For once again, if not guarded, in doing so our eyes drop from heaven to the earth.

Could it be that our sin, our struggles, our hang-ups do not diagnose our psychological disorder as much as they reveal a deficiency in our ability to adequately perceive God? When Adam and Eve sank their teeth into the delectable fruit they were not driven by hunger, nor were they driven by greed or lust; for at that point, sin was not in their DNA. They took the bait because, for a brief moment, they failed to see God as He is. They forgot who He was. We are talking about two people who had biblically recorded interaction with God. We are not talking about unbelievers. We are talking about friends of God who, in a moment, felt God wasn't enough. They wanted something more than Him.

In an odd way, acts of sin and internal sin serve as signposts, offering opportunity to rethink God and take another look to see what it is we have been missing in Him. The indictment of our sin is that we do not find God satisfying enough—however brief the moment of indiscretion. My sin is a statement that God isn't adequate for me. Why is extramarital sex a sin? It is a mere physical act to the scientific world. But to those designed for divine intimacy, it can become an illegitimate pleasure replacement for God. Why is the love of money so vile? The affection we hold for money states this currency can accomplish something for my soul that God cannot. Do our acts of sin grieve the Lord? Yes, with certainty. But could the greater grief of the Father be found in our lack of trust? If I struggle to trust Him, I must not be fully convinced He loves me. If I am not convinced He loves me, then clearly I have doubts about His goodness. Maybe the great grief sin elicits in the heart of God is that somewhere in our mind His true nature, His identity, has been misrepresented and He is seen as less than He really is. I am a daddy to a couple of beautiful kids. When they disobey me, I am frustrated. But to doubt me as a good daddy? That is heartbreaking.

With sin now in the world, we must approach it more aggressively for I can assure you its intent is aggressive. The first literal mention of the word "sin" is found in Genesis 4:7

> You will be accepted if you do what is right. But if you refuse to do what is right, then watch out! Sin is crouching at the door, eager to control you. But you must subdue it and be its master (Genesis 4:7).

God does not communicate sin as an action. Sin is not a behavior pattern. His admonition to Cain (the murdering son) was that *sin is an entity*. Sin was personified as a being or force that was intent on control. Sin doesn't put us on delicate strings like a marionette. Sin looks for a cockpit in our soul to slowly manipulate our life. Sin is the blinder affecting the whole by disrupting our perspective. Like God, sin has a dream. The insidious dream of sin is to control us to the degree that eviction from the pleasure of God is inevitable. We, it seems, spend much of our lives trying to stop sinning. Don't misinterpret what I am saying. Yes, we have actions that are sinful. Paul commands the believers of Corinth to "stop sinning" (1 Corinthians 15:34). However, one does not simply "stop sinning." Yes, self-control is a vital attribute. Paul tells the Galatians that self-control is actually a fruit of the Spirit of God (Galatians 5:22-23). Self-control is a grace imparted to the believer as it relates to overcoming sin, which is dependent upon our connectivity to the Spirit of God. Many a man and woman have borne the weight of disappointment and frustration after repeatedly failing to attain victory over a particular pattern. What if we have been contending against those sins inappropriately?

Will power and self-discipline have always been cumbersome to me. This is due, in part, because I have a personality type that is not naturally regimented. The notion of will power strikes me as very self-reliant. The phrase "will power" itself is a nod to strength in the flesh. It is quite possible for someone who doesn't believe in Jesus to abstain from drunkenness, fornication, telling lies, being mean, or murder. All of those arenas can be conquered through sheer determination and human effort. However, to not lust, not hate, not harbor racism, not walk in fear or be jealous requires something beyond trained behavior. Sin must be defeated not only in action, but at the core of a heart.

At times, we grow overly satisfied and self-congratulatory because we do not behave as the "heathen" do. However, is the value of our good behavior diminished if inwardly we are not much different? An underlying current throughout this book is true freedom, not merely the appearance of freedom. When the lights have been turned out, the TV shut down, and the conversation with others ceases, and we are left alone with ourselves, are we truly free? It is possible that one can will himself to outward expressions of liberty but be lacking in the total freedom Christ has made available. Here is a truth based on my experiences in ministry: We have a plethora of wonderful people in the body of Christ who behave like very good Christians and are lovely to be around, but inside they are a tangled mess of lust, doubt, anger, disappointment, despair, fear, insecurity, you name it. How does one combat this? It is one thing to deal with the very tangible enemy of fornication or murder. It is altogether a different challenge to wage war against the more abstract parts of our soul. The reality is that tangible sin behaviors are a direct result of our inner struggle. Once again, how do we attain victory?

> The Word gave life to everything that was created, and
> his life brought light to everyone. The light shines in

the darkness, and the darkness can never extinguish it
(John 1:4-5).

We have swung our swords at the darkness to no avail. I can personally attest that the fist of fury directed at the darkness in me has repeatedly failed to bring the darkness into submission. Darkness cannot be grabbed and taken hold of. John gives us this picture of Christ's victory, and within the analogy we find the folly of much of our sin-management church culture. We have concocted strategies to eradicate our sin and propagated them from pulpits as surefire methods. We have erroneously enlisted the human will and the restructuring of our surrounding amenities to overthrow an eternal illness. We have focused much of our preaching, teaching, and energy on symptom management. For many, we have not seen the manifestation of Christ's victory. Instead we have learned increasingly how to manage our darkness.

It is the person who has a proclivity to view pornography who is trying incredibly hard to no longer look at pornography. In an effort to not view pornography the person enlists an accountability partner. The accountability partner is not helping the person kill lust. The accountability partner is an outside source (not named Jesus) who we would be ashamed to disappoint. One hopes the embarrassment of having to tell someone "I looked at porn" will be an adequate deterrent. The problem is that one can lie to the accountability partner. In continued efforts to not look at pornography the individual deletes the Internet from their smartphone, puts blocks on their computer, and turns off the cable. Yet the imagination cannot be disconnected so easily. I sincerely admire the efforts we go through to push sin out of our lives. However, darkness cannot be handled. Darkness only responds to one thing— light. The light that shines into the darkness that is incapable of being extinguished.

It is elementary but revelatory. Darkness is defined by the absence of light. Darkness is not even its own thing. It is only allowed existence in the places where light is not presently shining. Darkness is weak. How embarrassing for darkness that its very definition is derived from its enemy and the lack thereof? We have made darkness this ever-present, daunting foe. John communicates darkness as completely subject to *the* light that is Jesus—the same Christ who quickens our mortal bodies. How do we confront the darkness in our life? By turning on the light. Darkness shrouds our ability to see clearly. Light opens the eyes of our understanding, giving us a completely different perspective on the same set of circumstances. If you have a darkness problem, it is conquered by looking at the light. Look at Jesus! Stare at Jesus! Let Jesus in! Stop trying to keep out the darkness on your own. Instead, focus on the light! Instead of studying darkness and trying to bolster ourselves against it, begin the journey of more accurately perceiving Jesus.

As one who has preached many sermons, I have come to a rather humbling conclusion. I can repeatedly identify, label, and instruct others to "stop sinning," but rarely is this method effective. No matter how "on" or "anointed" my preaching is, once the hearers have left the sound of my voice and returned to the world from whence they came, having heard the admonition to *stop* is of little value. We expend copious amounts of energy and emotional cache in our efforts to "stop sinning." Do you want to hear what may be considered a ridiculous declaration, if it is not accompanied by sufficient revelation?

Stop trying to "stop sinning"!

Sin is not conquered through management. Sin has already been conquered in the mangled flesh attached to the cross, the seed of heaven being plunged into the depths, and the darkened tomb being flooded with the third-day light. Jesus is not *an* answer (as cliché as that may sound). Jesus is *the* answer. Jesus is Yahweh's response to sin, His unequivocally perfect response that breaks the back of the crouching control freak. As simply as I can state it: Immense focus on Jesus pushes back the darkness that encroaches on your soul. Jesus has conquered your foe. Increased revelation of God the Father, God the Son, and God the Holy Spirit satisfies what gnaws at the soul and overturns the detrimental craving inside. To see the light is to diminish the allure and intrigue of the darkness. To see Jesus correctly changes everything. To fix our eyes on what He has done, as opposed to living under the overwhelming weight of what we must do but will never fully achieve, is the elixir for a free heart.

> To fix our eyes on what He has done, as opposed to living under the overwhelming weight of what we must do but will never fully achieve, is the elixir for a free heart.

CHAPTER 6: PERCEIVE

God sent a man, John the Baptist, to tell about the light so that everyone might believe because of his testimony. John himself was not the light; he was simply a *witness* to tell about the light. The one who is the true light, who gives light to everyone, was coming into the world. He came into the very world he created, but the world didn't recognize him. He came to his own people, and even they rejected him (John 1:6-11).

John, the author of this gospel, seems to be implying that seeing Jesus clearly is not to be taken for granted. There was a segment of the population 2,000 years ago that had an immense amount of information and knowledge about the coming Messiah, but they were inadequate in their ability to perceive Jesus as the Answer to their waiting. They couldn't see Jesus clearly. John the Baptist perceived. The disciples perceived. The religious establishment did not perceive. These verses are a cautionary tale of two groups looking at the exact same thing yet seeing something completely different. Please don't miss the path we are on. This is not a random diversion. You have a religious class who were full of intellectual information and well versed in the expectations of the system. Yet the system was (and still is) completely inadequate in confronting and nullifying the grip of sin and darkness. Darkness (sin) is not intimidated by a system of beliefs and routines centered on a set of rules or a high volume of information about a spiritual subject. Darkness is only affected when Jesus is looked upon, perceived appropriately, and pursued genuinely.

Satan, who is the god of this world, has blinded the minds of those who don't believe (2 Corinthians 4:4a).

Why has he blinded the minds of the unbeliever? What is he trying to prevent them from *seeing*?

> They are unable to see the glorious light of the Good News. They don't understand this message about the glory of Christ, who is the exact likeness of God (2 Corinthians 4:4b).

Paul has an unusual turn of phrase in this verse. *Blinded* (which speaks of vision) *the minds* (which speaks of thinking). Paul was speaking about the transition from what you see to how you perceive. He is speaking of a shift from information to revelation, which completely alters one's life function. How is sin defeated in our lives? How is the darkness pushed back? It is not enough to position yourself in a setting in which you have a great deal of information dispensed into your brain. It is not enough to wear the accoutrements of cultural Christianity and look the part of a believer through Christlike actions. The journey to true freedom is found in the personal pursuit of the person of Jesus. It is about knowing Him and not stopping at knowing *of* Him. I know this may come across as incredibly common. You may have been around church enough to know you must have a relationship with the Lord. Maybe we should be asking whether or not we are more like the religious class of the day or John the Baptist and the disciples. The difference was that the former had a wealth of understanding *about* the Messiah. The latter actually recognized and *knew* the Messiah.

The journey to true freedom is found in the personal pursuit of the person of Jesus.

The friction is that to truly know Jesus is to have your world wrecked. The religious class refused to embrace Jesus to the full because He came with a kingdom directly threatening to their status, authority, control, routine, finances, lifestyle, comfort, preferences, and esteem. They were looking for a Messiah who would exalt them and their agenda. They weren't quite sure what to do with a Messiah who came to establish a kingdom, which deposed their way of life.

Can I pause for a moment? Is it possible that we look at our precious Savior much the same? We like a version of Jesus that gives us a path to wealth, comfort, favor, success, and blessing. I am guilty as charged. I like the idea of plugging in the principles of the Bible and it resulting in the above. Yet we've already established that the dream God has for us has little to do with those results. Instead, it is primarily about us and Him being in continuous connection. It is about *abiding*. Those accessories are a by-product of connectivity.

The answer for your sin, your struggle, and your frustration is not to put on more steam in the effort department. The resolution you are seeking is found in Jesus. The challenge of Jesus is that we do not have the luxury of being casual with Him. The struggle of much of modern society Christianity is the leaning toward a very neutral, casual version of faith. We don't have the liberty of saying *I am cool with Jesus, but I am going to compartmentalize Him to certain areas of my life.* We would never literally say to Jesus: "Stay right here in this spot and don't cross that threshold of my life." However, it is imperative we search the soul and ask the tough questions about how much access we have granted Jesus. We (myself included) are so prone to put up walls and start rationalizing why we aren't as intimate with Him in certain areas of our life.

> The life of following Jesus is one in which we embrace consistent confrontation of our comforts and preferences.

The life of following Jesus is one in which we embrace consistent confrontation of our comforts and preferences. I say this not alluding to living in a hut or selling all our possessions and carrying a cross across the nation. Rather it is inviting Jesus into our life in such a way that all our prerecorded answers and explanations, which bring us comfort and fit our agenda, are laid aside in pursuit of better knowing the ways of His heart. It is "Teach me *Your* ways, oh, Lord." It is not, "Here are *my* ways and we will figure out how *You* fit into that worldview." We have a confusing view of our salvation. Even our verbiage hinders our thinking. We say things like: "Invite Jesus into your heart," and in doing so, we position ourselves as the one with control. Think about how the relationships between Jesus and the disciples were initiated. Jesus said, "Come, follow Me." They responded to His call. Salvation, a life in Christ, has never been about us offering an invitation to Jesus. It has always been about us hearing His invitation and responding. We are not inviting Jesus into our world, into our perspective. Jesus is inviting us into His world and His perspective. My faith is not about constructing my world and figuring out how Jesus fits therein. My faith is about following Jesus into a kingdom that defies the logic, reasoning, and systems of this world. My faith is about discovering, through relationship, how to more consistently and overtly sync up my world with His. The "problem" with God is that He is too big to fit into our world.

Truth be told, He already squeezed Himself into our world once in the form of a man who can now sympathize with us as a result of His human experience. He made Himself fit into this world once so He could grant us access into His world. He isn't fitting into our world any longer. Instead, He is elevating us into His.

How can we possibly elevate into His world?

CHAPTER 7: HISTORY AND GEOGRAPHY

Our theology, our view of God and the world around us, is filtered through lenses. These lenses have been accrued through our history and geography.

This thought gives us some perspective on the unique dichotomy between John the Baptist and those who did not recognize Jesus for who He was—the One. The vast majority of my childhood and the entirety of my teen years were lived under the roof of a home built by my dad. Our family had a respectable, but modest, income for most of my upbringing. Both of my parents were raised in farming families that would likely be considered closer to the poverty level today. My hometown was a farming community with a few factories, which provided jobs. However, many people had to travel forty-five minutes to an hour away for work in nearby Memphis. We played baseball, hunted, fished, and on occasion I ran the cotton fields surrounding my house. Our town in western Tennessee lacked a booming economy and was simple in the way every small town is simple. There was racial tension, nepotism, poverty, and not-so-well-kept secrets. There was also a sense of community pride and togetherness. It was our town. I grew up attending an Assembly of God church that had roughly 200 people in attendance. I went to church camps and conferences. When I was in seventh grade, my parents divorced and I lived in the aforementioned house with my mom and sister. My dad stayed in town and we spent Sundays at his house after we were done with church. I eventually went to Bible college and have lived multiple places since.

LET YOUR HEART GO FREE

My worldview has been shaped by that upbringing and those surroundings. Growing up in a rural town in the Southeastern region of the United States in the Northern and Western hemispheres shaped how I see the world and continues to do so to this day. How I see race, money, government, politics, and religion is all filtered through the information above and so much more. No matter how much I try to ignore it, my perception of God, how I receive Him, and how I approach Him is affected by my history and geography. Does this make me a bad person? Of course not! I had no more say in being raised in Tennessee than I did in having blue eyes. But it is irresponsible of me to dismiss the idea that my theological vision has filters and lenses through which I see. I can see some aspects of God more clearly because of my personal history but other aspects, not as well. It's not only our geography but our experiences that filter our vision. If you were abandoned, abused, impoverished, sick, or bullied, or if you were wealthy, went on vacations, were loved well by your dad, and had stability in your life—those experiences all shaped the narrative of God in your heart. What is your story? What has been your geography? Dare you ask the question of just how much your view of Jesus has been filtered through those lenses? I say we have no choice; otherwise, our history and geography become the captains of our soul instead of Jesus.

> ## Like it or not, our ability to perceive God, to see Jesus well, is in contention with much of our personal history.

Like it or not, our ability to perceive God, to see Jesus well, is in contention with much of our personal history. We read this account in the previous chapter, but let's re-look at ourselves, considering the filters over our spiritual eyes.

> God sent a man, John the Baptist, to tell about the light
> so that everyone might believe because of his testimony.
> John himself was not the light; he was simply a *witness*

to tell about the light. The one who is the true light, who gives light to everyone, was coming into the world. He came into the very world he created, but the world didn't recognize him. He came to his own people, and even they rejected him (John 1:6-11, emphasis mine).

Before we talk about John, what about "his own people…even they rejected him"? The reality was that every human in the earth at that time was "his own people." But this pertained to the Jewish people all the more; they had lived in covenant with the triune God for multiple millennia. They were privy to the "your son will crush the head of the serpent" part of Genesis. They sang as hymns the prophetic psalms foretelling a coming great King. They were well versed in the prophetic declarations of Isaiah and Jeremiah about the coming Messiah. They had a clue sheet helping them identify the suffering Servant who would alleviate their pain. If they had simply paused, reflected, and looked a little more closely, they would have noticed Jesus checked off all the boxes of their long awaited hope. But they didn't. Sure, there were 5,000 on the hillside as He broke bread and distributed fish. Of course, there were the throngs of people tossing cloaks and palm branches before Him the week before Passover. Yet even those who had an inkling of His eternal legitimacy took a step back when circumstances changed and identifying with Him became less beneficial.

How did they miss Jesus? How did they miss this brilliant philosophical intellectual? How did they miss this dead-raising, water-walking, crowd-feeding, sick-woman-healing, storm-stopping, and demon-exorcising Embodiment of love, kindness, and generosity? How do you reject Jesus? It seems patently absurd to me as I type and probably does to you as you read. When reading the Bible, we have a tendency to insert ourselves into the stories as the hero. We read ourselves into the part of the faithful, obedient, astute, unwavering, and committed. However, it is wise to also read ourselves into the role of the villain, the one who got it wrong. More times than not, I find I would be more likely to fall into that category than the more noble one. Could I have been "one of his own" who "rejected him"? I want to throw my hands up, lift my voice defensively, and exclaim "No way!"

How did they miss Him? Massive books full of Jewish cultural context have been written to explain their error. I will keep it simple. Their personal history and geography blurred their vision. By the time Jesus stepped into the public eye, there was scarcely anyone alive living in the region of Judea who knew anything but the overarching Roman rule. Israel was not its own state. They were under the government of Rome with its taxation, laws, and slowly encroaching culture. The religious class of the Jewish people through the generations became intertwined with political affairs and hopes of a Rescuer to remove the thumb of Rome. Their history and geography caused them to place particular ideals on the coming Messiah, shaping Him into what they felt the Sent One would have to be in order to accomplish the task at hand. Along the way, they had become accustomed to some measure of comfort and nobility among the people and anticipated a Messiah who would affirm and work in conjunction with their status in the Jewish world. These filters, among many, so clouded their ability to perceive that instead of hoisting Jesus on their shoulders, they hoisted Him up onto the cross.

Could I miss Him? If He were to show up on the scene today, could we miss Him? Would my political persuasion cloud my view when He did something contrary to what I think is appropriate? Would my ideas about money cause me to dismiss Him if He contradicted my thought patterns in that area? Would I miss Him because of race, appearance, fashion, or some other tangible reason? Would my Southern code cause me to misidentify the One sent from heaven? Today, does some of my personal history and geographical influence create thought patterns that make it difficult for me to perceive and receive Jesus well? Honestly, I'm sure this happens way more than I care to admit.

Fortunately, we have John the Baptist as a sign of hope, and the reality that it is possible to see Jesus well in spite of all we have known and experienced.

CHAPTER 8: THE WITNESS

I f personal history and geography affected so many in their ability to perceive and receive Jesus, what enabled John to see? Did he not grow up in the same history and geography as so many others who missed Jesus? Certainly, but something else, or should I say Someone else, was at work in John. We have read it a couple of times already. John 1:8 tells us John was a *witness* to tell about the light that is Jesus.

The one word that may be the most cringe-inducing in all of Christendom is the word *witness*. It summons up angst, stress, shame, fear, and occasionally self-loathing. How many times have we heard the pounding of a pulpit, followed by the guilt-laden challenge that we must witness to those around us, and if we do not we have failed the Lord and doomed those poor souls to the lake of fire for eternity? I will readily admit that in my younger years I was notorious for berating the teenagers under my care with the necessity of witnessing. If I plunge fully into the waters of honesty, I'm sure my motivation for doing so was a mixture of concern for the lost and a desire for increased attendance in my youth ministry, but that is a conversation for another day in another book.

I wonder if we have, to some degree, misappropriated the actual definition of the term *witness*. Let me explain.

> John himself was not the light; he was simply a *witness*
> to tell about the light (John 1:8).

Have you ever noticed the distinction in these verses between "witness" and "tell"? There is another verse in the Bible in which the word *witness* is used.

> But you will receive power when the Holy Spirit comes
> upon you. And you will be my *witnesses*, telling people
> about me everywhere—in Jerusalem, throughout Judea,
> in Samaria, and to the ends of the earth (Acts 1:8).

What if the word *witness* does not quite mean the same thing as "tell"? What if the word *witness* means something of much greater substance? I submit to you this is not only possible, it is a reality. The usage of "witness" and "witnesses" found in John 1:8 and Acts 1:8 are linked to the Greek word *martus*, which is a word closely connected with our English word *martyr*.[6] *Martus* is used in a couple of other instances to directly indicate someone who died for the cause of Christ. In both of the above translations a distinction is made between being a witness (a martyr) and telling others the good news of the gospel. Being a witness and telling are not the same thing. They are two parts to the equation, not equal parts. There is a common component that syncs these two passages with one another—Holy Spirit.

In Acts 1:8 there was a soon coming promised One who would empower us to *martus* that we might tell everyone, everywhere. John the Baptist was filled with Holy Spirit while still being formed in his mother's womb (see Luke 1:15). Just for good measure, there is another instance that beautifully paints this portrait.

Jesus—rising from the current, garments soaked and clinging, beads of water glistening in the sun, hair dripping, eyes upward, voice of heaven booming with acceptance and validation, and a descending dove— Holy Spirit settling on the One who would serve Himself up as the quintessential martyr.

Holy Spirit plays this unique and important role in our lives. In John 16, Jesus tells His disciples of His nearing departure, but He adds that He will leave behind a Comforter. The English Standard Versions calls Him Helper. Regarding the role of Holy Spirit, Jesus says:

---

6. James Strong, "Strong's Greek: 3144. μάρτυς (martus) -- a Witness," accessed May 03, 2018, http://biblehub.com/greek/3144.htm.

> He (Holy Spirit) will convict the world of its sin, and of God's righteousness…The world's sin is that it refuses to believe in me…When the Spirit of truth comes, he will guide you into all truth…He will bring me glory by telling you whatever he receives from me (John 16:8-9,13-14, addition mine).

The most familiar synopsis of those verses is that the primary assignment of Holy Spirit is to reveal Jesus. Therefore, John, full of the Spirit, was able to perceive Jesus. To be a witness is much more about beholding than it is about telling. You cannot give an adequate account of something you have not perceived well for yourself.

It was this infilling of Holy Spirit which enabled John to see Jesus more clearly. It did not come through the filter of "How does He benefit me? How does He affect my reputation? What is this going to cost me? How does His agenda play out with my own agenda? Do Jesus' dreams mesh with my personal dreams?" No! John saw Jesus for who He was:

> Look! The Lamb of God who takes away the sin of the world! (John 1:29)

He saw no coattails to ride on for personal validation. He saw no momentum to follow for personal acclaim. We know from the rest of the gospel account that John was eventually beheaded for his unwavering prophetic testimony of Jesus and his contention with the morality of the governmental authority, Herod. Emboldened by the Spirit, he was a martyr because he saw Jesus unfiltered.

Peter likely presents us with our best template for understanding. In Matthew 16, we find Peter rebuking Jesus because the Messiah's mission does not fit his agenda. In the dark hours of the garden of Gethsemane, we find Peter wielding his sword in vengeance and anger, bringing harm to Malchus's ear. Once again, Peter is lacking understanding and reacting to his circumstances in a carnal manner. In Peter we have a conflicted man. In one moment he makes lofty proclamations of his undying loyalty, but in the darkness of a trumped up trial he cowers in the shadows with denial dripping from his lips. From the crowing of the rooster, he transitions to a place of hiding with his fellow social pariahs. Yes, they pray and fellowship, but they also settle into the security of hiding, fearing exposure to the outside world will result in their demise much like their Master experienced days before.

The weary band of followers was steeped in the mode of self-preservation. Were they justified? To some degree, the answer is yes, for Jesus commanded them to wait. In Acts 2, as the sound of wind rushed into their upper room and tongues of fire settled over their heads, a dramatic change took place within their hearts. A people concealed by the closed windows of a secluded room suddenly threw open the shutters and allowed the outside world to hear the sound of their experience. Peter—short of Judas, the most tragic of the disciples, the one with the most reasonable excuse to take a back seat—stepped onto a terrace. Weeks before he had feared for his life to the degree that he renounced the Son of God, but under the influence of Holy Spirit he stepped into the light, exposing himself to possible assassination. His days of fear and self-protection had come to an end, and a journey started that would ultimately lead to him hanging upside down, in the clutches of his opposition, dying the death of crucifixion on a cross.

What happened? Holy Spirit's deep engagement and powerful infilling happened. Read the New Testament. Those connected to the life and power of Holy Spirit lived with an abandon that often led to an unnatural demise. They were possessed with the Spirit of heaven to the degree that they regarded His heart and mission of greater value than their own lives. Simply reading and pondering the epic display of sacrifice and surrender of the early disciples has an almost romantic air. What does this mean in my hour of oxygen consumption in the earth? The same Holy Spirit who filled John the Baptist in the womb, descended on the baptized Messiah, and baptized 120 weary followers has remained in the domain of the earth through the generations and eagerly anticipates a similar life with you. He longs to immerse you in Himself that you may become a martyr to the ways of this world. Holy Spirit has come that we may cease in our cravings of the flesh. He has come for the purpose of dealing a deathblow to self-centeredness. He has come to eradicate our love affair with a system that does not love us back. He has come to reveal.

The Holy Spirit seeks to intertwine with our nature with such depth that the lenses acquired through our history and geography are removed. Holy Spirit, in some cases instantly and in others progressively, converts us into increasingly pure vision. Our spirit was transitioned from death to life upon conversion, and our soul is being transitioned into the likeness of the Lord where we begin to operate more as citizens of heaven than as citizens of our upbringing.

> The Holy Spirit seeks to intertwine with our nature with such depth that the lenses acquired through our history and geography are removed.

I will take the importance of the Holy Spirit a step further. Ponder this thought: The disciples spent roughly three years fully invested in Jesus' earthly ministry. They were firsthand observers to His every action, habit, and teaching. Three years with Jesus. Three years with the Son of God. Yet at the conclusion of His human form assignment, Jesus made it clear that the disciples having been with Jesus was not enough. Sure, they slept near Him, shared meals, walked roads, eavesdropped on prayers, experienced miracles, and heard almost every word. Yet according to Jesus, this was not sufficient. Something else was required for them to fulfill the mission. Someone else was needed in order to flesh out this kingdom life. I would think three years with Jesus would be enough to set us up for the rest of our lives. But my thinking is severely limited, and Jesus is a Mystery who has been around since before all things. Three years was not enough time. It was not internally invasive to the degree that God designed. Walking with Jesus in physical form was insufficient according to Jesus Himself. This kingdom life requires the intimate assistance of One who has been with Jesus since before all things. Holy Spirit revealed Jesus in a way those three years fell short of doing. Jesus never intended to be received outside the work of Holy Spirit, His Co-laborer and Partner in fellowship since before all things.

Holy Spirit reveals Jesus in such a way that people transform from being self-preserving, narcissistic lovers of this world into being martyrs, dying in their affections for the things this world offers. I can't say I am the ultimate authority on this topic, but if you were to ask me what the primary function of Holy Spirit in the life of a believer is, I would say it this way:

Holy Spirit reveals Jesus in such a way that we are continually decreasing in our love for the things of this world and continually increasing in our love for the things of God. Holy Spirit helps us see Jesus well and, in the process, reshapes our view of the world. How does this work? Surely by now you know I don't have all the answers. Like so many aspects of faith, it is a mystery—a never-ending discovery. Peter was a believer, but Holy Spirit transformed him into a martyr. We have to admit, all of our personal history and familiar geography over time creates common thought patterns in our mind. The longer those thought patterns remain, the more deeply entrenched they become. Ultimately, they become ruts, difficult to get out of and confining in our ability to perceive God more clearly and receive all He has made available. One of the primary roles of Holy Spirit, in conjunction with Scripture, is to fill in those ruts. Following Jesus, to a large degree, is a journey of allowing Holy Spirit to remove all of those filters we have accumulated through the years of our history and geography. We must be willing to allow them to be challenged and removed, one at a time, as we gain an increasingly clearer view of the One. The better we see Him, the less the world has appeal. The weaker the allure of the world, the freer the heart gets.

The infilling of the Holy Spirit, dialogue with the Holy Spirit, and opening our hearts to Holy Spirit transforms us. Over time, silver and gold and all other shiny things lose their luster in the brilliant light of Jesus. Those filters diminish His radiant glow. Holy Spirit removes the lenses, fills in the illegitimate thought ruts, and helps us think anew—

better, like heaven. You can't talk about or see Jesus well without Holy Spirit. Fortunately, Holy Spirit is available to help.

CHAPTER 9: BABEL

For quite some time now, I have felt Holy Spirit is the great antidote for Babel. Throughout Scripture there are clear antagonists that are in direct conflict with the ways of heaven and the kingdom of God. One such adversary, interwoven from Genesis to Revelation, is Babylon. Whether referring to the specific geographical location or a spirit at work in the earth, the ways of Babel routinely contend with the heart of heaven. You may wonder why I am jumping outside of the framework of John 1:1-13. It's because I have a suspicion the same filters that propelled "his own" to reject Jesus were prevalent in the city of Babel early in Genesis. I also know too well how those filters have obscured my view along the way and kept my heart bound.

> At one time all the people of the world spoke the *same language* and used the same words. As the people migrated to the east, they found a plain in the land of Babylonia and settled there. They began saying to each other, "Let's make bricks and harden them with fire." (In this region bricks were used instead of stone, and tar was used for mortar.) *Then they said, "Come, let's build a great city for ourselves with a tower that reaches into the sky. This will make us famous and keep us from being scattered all over the world."* But the Lord came down to look at the city and the tower the people were building. "Look!" he said. "The people are united, and they all speak the same language. After this, *nothing they set out to do will be impossible for them!* Come, let's go down and confuse the people with different languages.

Then they won't be able to understand each other." In that way, the Lord scattered them all over the world, and they stopped building the city. That is why the city was called Babel, because that is where the Lord confused the people with different languages. In this way he scattered them all over the world (Genesis 11:1-9, emphasis mine).

One chapter after the great flood, mankind had insufficiently learned the lesson. Disappointingly, as I read of the men and women of Babel, it seems I may have fit in there better than I wish. The people of the region of Babylonia (and it seems the whole earth) spoke one language. Theologians may argue about the nature of this account. Was it literal or metaphorical? It is difficult to fathom a point in human history in which everyone spoke one language, yet we are left with this statement in Scripture; and like many times in the life of faith, we must accept what seems like a mystery. This shared vocabulary created among them a synergy that seems almost foreign to us in modern times. It created a camaraderie, unity, an accord that empowered them to defy their limitations. Their common dialect forged them into a force capable of superseding their individual weaknesses and strengths.

God Himself made the declaration: *"After this, nothing they set out to do will be impossible for them!"* On the surface this sounds like a resounding endorsement from heaven. For those of us who have been fitted with an Americanized filter, we can easily misinterpret what the Father is saying as a stamp of approval. *"Hey! God said **nothing** is **impossible** for us!"* It sounds like an incredible ad. It sounds similar to a verse we modern-day believers toss around almost casually: *"I can do everything through Christ, who gives me strength"* (Philippians 4:13). Maybe it's just me, but have you ever noticed how often the immense vastness of God and His unfathomable mysteries gets broken down into clichéd sound bites that fit neatly within the context of our self-focused, personal advancement existence? Take the aforementioned extracted nugget from Philippians 4:13 as an example. It sounds so American. It sounds so right. Is it possible that Paul was not offering up a catchy slogan for the industry of Christianity to use as a nice pick me up? Paul preceded the "I can do all things" with:

> I know how to live on almost nothing or with everything.
> I have learned the secret of living in every situation,
> whether it is with a full stomach or empty, with plenty or
> little (Philippians 4:12).

Paul was saying, "I have been initiated into the mysteries of God through the struggle of life. This initiation has taught me how to be at peace, how to be content, how to have joy when it is painful, how to be humble when I'm in a moment of triumph, how to have a heart postured in a way that is honorable to God regardless of the season. In the isolation and desolation of winter my heart is pure and at peace. In the harvest of fall, as I count my bounty, my heart holds no hubris. I can do all of that through Christ who strengthens me!"

We radically cheapen the wonder-working power of the gospel when we boil it down to overused platitudes. "I can do all things through Christ who gives me strength," when ripped from its context, loses its truth. I am 6 feet 3 inches and 155 pounds. I will never, regardless of the amount of work I invest, become a professional football player. My genetics are not predisposed to great athletic feats. As a teenager I loved playing sports. I once went to the name brand nutrition store and bought two containers of "shake mix" that guaranteed twenty pounds of weight gain per container. First, the stuff tasted putrid. I had to quote "I can do all things through Christ" just to convince myself I could choke a shake down. Second, I didn't gain a pound.

My point in this diatribe is simple:

If we are not careful we will "red, white, and blue" the gospel to the point that we start to believe God is in the business of making our dreams come true. It is important to ask the difficult questions about our life's dreams.

- What percentage of my dreams are self-centered?

- What percentage of my dreams are focused on attaining earthly possessions?

- What percentage of my dreams are about impressing other people?

- What percentage of my dreams require little of the supernatural of God and are heavily dependent on my own talent and abilities?

> ## If we are not careful we will "red, white, and blue" the gospel to the point that we start to believe God is in the business of making our dreams come true.

In a moment of transparency, I have come to discover that too many of my dreams through the years have had the appearance of nobility on the surface, but upon closer inspection resemble the culture of Babel. Those men and women declared the following:

"Let's make a great city for ourselves" (as opposed as for the Lord).

"This will make us famous."

"This will keep us from being scattered."

These people used the labor of their lives, their ingenuity, their intellect, the sweat of their brow, and their hours of effort and energy to build something for themselves. They invested heavily in their own delight and pleasure. They expended themselves for themselves. They did so in order to gain the admiration and respect of others. They craved fame. They wanted to be noticed and admired. They subtly desired to be the topic of conversation and the object of others' jealousy. They also longed for security, convenience, and comfort. They endeavored to establish a place of residence in which they could have what they needed within relatively easy reach.

In essence, the people of Babel hungered for a life in which God was a nice amenity but not a minute-by-minute necessity. They aspired to live on the earth, partaking of its wares, striving to eliminate the need for faith, thus allowing them the convenience of fitting God into neat compartments. They pursued the luxuries of the earth, all the while relegating God to the status of an add-on. God was a perk, not the pursuit.

Be mindful. The great flood was ushered in by the brazen wickedness of mankind.

> The Lord observed the extent of human wickedness on the earth, and he saw that everything they thought or imagined was consistently and totally evil (Genesis 6:5).

However, in Babel there is no mention of lewdness, drunkenness, overt sexuality, or blatant external sin. We have no reference to the debauchery of pre-flood earth. No, this darkness was possibly more insidious because it came disguised as something that had no surface appearance of evil. The people were busy; they were industrious little beavers. They were hard workers, good leaders, committed to their craft, giving their best, going the extra mile, and dreaming big. Does this sound familiar? It should, because it is Americana at its finest. How strategic of our enemy, that he would so effectively camouflage core elements of the flesh into the fabric of our culture, lulling us into believing the pursuit of our life and the purpose of God are our own happiness and comfort. How clever to make building for ourselves noble in our society, to make it an admired, better than the next person, comfortable, safe existence. All the while he is duping us into feeding our carnality at the expense of a better way.

This is a filter that hinders our ability to see Jesus well. It causes us to search for legitimate validation in illegitimate arenas. It is the filter of self. It is the filter of being concerned with how we are viewed by others, which is in absolute conflict with a free heart. It is the filter of convenience. The people who rejected Jesus missed Him because of these filters and many others. Some of the lenses over their eyes were no fault of their own. They were their inheritance from living in the region or their teachers or parents. Nonetheless, whether earned or unfairly received, these kinds of filters cloud visibility and lead us down the path of the religious class who failed to celebrate Jesus too. Let me be clear.

LET YOUR HEART GO FREE

I am not on any pinnacle far removed from the struggle. I am a fellow sojourner in need of internal reformation. This reformation comes from the power of Holy Spirit, who is in the process of removing the filters from my eyes that I might witness well.

We need Holy Spirit.

I have always been intrigued by doctrinal certainty. More specifically, I am fascinated with our tendency to embrace some layers of mystery in God and dismiss others as being too difficult or uncomfortable or illogical. I want to reiterate—the Holy Spirit infilling, empowerment, and leading are available in this moment. If you have narrowed your emphasis of Holy Spirit out of doctrinal loyalty or fear of the unknown, do you think it would be reasonable to ask Holy Spirit about Himself? If *"the Spirit teaches you everything you need to know,"* He might have something to say to you about how He perceives His role in your life. And to my Pentecostal friends, could it be you've missed some of the mystery of Holy Spirit in the certainty of what you've always heard? Could it be you are indeed commissioned to "tell" but the role of Holy Spirit in this process begins with the death of self?

Holy Spirit reveals Jesus.

As Jesus is revealed, the enticement of sin is diminished.

As Jesus is revealed, self-centeredness dies a slow death.

As Jesus is revealed, our soul is freed.

As Jesus is revealed, the harbinger of fear and intimidation is broken.

As Jesus is revealed, the gospel is told.

Holy Spirit?

He converts me from cultural Christian to spiritual martyr.

CHAPTER 10: CRAVING

Perceiving and receiving Jesus well (becoming a witness) is, in part, instantaneous and, in part, process. It is important to diminish neither the sudden capabilities of God nor the process of God. Both *suddenly* and *everyday* have a beautiful kinship. Though seemingly opposite, they tend to work in unison.

Both *suddenly* and *everyday* have a beautiful kinship.

When I was in college, I loved soda. In my cinder block, walled dorm room I had very few possessions. I had a bed, which was the property of the school, and a mattress upon which I lay that may have been there since the 1970s. However, the crown jewel of the room was my little refrigerator. Scripture says we are jars of clay and it is what is inside the jar that gives value. This could not have been more accurate in regard to this little brown refrigerator, for inside it was always stocked with the dew from Mount Hermon, carbonated goodness—soda. Those aluminum cans were a sign of refreshing and joy. It was not uncommon for me to roll over at 3:00 a.m., open the door to the little fridge, and grab a can of liquid happiness. I would chug it and go back to sleep. I drank so much soda that its caffeinated properties lost their effect. I had such a fondness for a particular brand of soda that I kept every empty can and sticky tacked them to the wall in my cell—I mean, dorm room.

I had rows and rows of cans hung as a decorative piece, commemorating my love affair. There were many rumors in those days of the effects of my soda of choice, especially on the male species. The buzz was that drinking too much of the beverage would inhibit one's ability to have children. I didn't care about having children. I wanted the soda. Those cautionary tales did nothing to curb my craving for a good, cold swig. And drink on I did. Until somewhere in my mid-twenties when I decided, after repeatedly hearing of the detrimental effects of soda, to stop drinking it. I am not saying it was the easiest thing to do. Anyone who has ever done something consistently for a long time is aware that breaking habits can be challenging. Fast forward to my current life. These days I spend my summers running "church camps" for teenagers and children. Because I am the leader of the camps, I have access to all the camp has available, which includes an unlimited supply of fountain drinks in the concession stand. If I chose to do so, I would have the liberty to walk over with a colorful paper cup, hold it under the fountain, and push the little trigger, causing that wonderful soda to flow forth. However, I have spent many weeks on that property without taking one single drink of my former favorite beverage of choice. Why? Somewhere along the way, my cravings changed. In recent years I have occasionally grabbed a soda and taken a sip. It tasted horrible to me. I no longer like the carbonation, the syrupy texture, or the overwhelming sugar. My craving has changed. As a result, my tastes have changed and what was once refreshing has now become undesirable. I have conquered soda. Next comes sweet iced tea—that's another, even steeper, mountain to climb.

> Like newborn babies, you must crave pure spiritual milk
> so that you will grow into a full experience of salvation.
> Cry out for this nourishment, now that you have had a
> taste of the Lord's kindness (1 Peter 2:2-3).

In a previous chapter I made the statement to stop trying to stop sinning. It creates an almost inescapable vortex that further fixes our focus on the sin as opposed to the splendor of the One. However, the spiritual expectation of holiness, purity, and not succumbing to temptation remains firmly in place for our own benefit. Therefore, it is imperative to take hold of what we crave that we may, as Peter says, grow into a full experience of salvation. Upon reading this, I am slowed almost to a standstill at the invitation Peter offers—a full experience of salvation. The implied idea is that some believers may be under the covering of the blood of Jesus and destined for an eternal rest in paradise but lacking in some way when it comes to the totality of the salvation experience. Peter was all too familiar with this concept. He was a believer in Jesus as well as an avid follower; yet outside the work of Holy Spirit, he found himself in compromise.

Peter alludes to an appropriate craving as a key component to the managing and enhancement of our spiritual life. At times we have viewed craving as this intense desire over which we have little control or influence. A craving is what it is, something from some unknown realm in our being. We spend our entire lives fighting with our cravings. Peter likely understood cravings a little differently. He seems to imply that it was possible to manipulate what we desire and to shape our appetite. As we established earlier, I have been some version of "saved" for the whole of my life. A lifetime of faith causes one to look a little deeper than what lies on the surface. If you spend decades as a follower of Jesus and you never ask yourself challenging questions, I wonder if you have actually met Jesus. My questions sound something like this:

> *"It is good I have established in my life a lack of drunkenness, a disdain for lies, and other outward acts of sin. However, how much do my internal thoughts and yearnings mesh more with the sinful nature than they do Holy Spirit?"*

The law of the Old Testament has an appeal because it was fixed on outward discipline and tangible markers for holiness and piety. However, this dispensation of grace ushered in by Jesus has reached deeper into the fabric of who we are than the Mosaic Law ever could. The Old Testament, on many fronts, was easy. There were 613 laws in the Torah, spelled out. There was a checklist of dos and don'ts—some of which seem odd in this modern era but nonetheless there were no gray areas. In the Old Testament I could, in theory, have disdain for my brother as long as I didn't harm him. I could have unruly affections for another woman as long as I didn't touch her. Yet Jesus pushed humanity into an era in which our core thinking and processing are as important as our outward expression—maybe more important. I say this as an often-frustrated Christian who knows the behavioral markers of our faith, but also knows the internal dialogue I have with my flesh. Through the years, it has been a joy when I have denied sin in the hour of temptation, but there is also the tension present that Jesus' work on the cross was substantial enough that this should no longer be a temptation—what am I missing? Why do I crave the wrong things? Why do I still yearn for sin? I've been at this long enough! Some of this stuff should be dead in me by now. It should be crucified with Christ.

In those moments we often lean on Paul's diatribe of, "I don't do what I want to do and I do what I don't want to do" (see Romans 7:15), using it as a means of justifying our improper cravings. It is easier to justify our desires by thinking, *I'm human, I'm flesh, and I'm flawed! Nobody is perfect, and hey! Look, Paul struggled too!* That is easier than it is to take the responsibility of managing our cravings. Before your frustrations start bubbling to the surface, I want you to know that this is not meant to heap condemnation on anyone. Remember, these are questions I routinely ask myself. Once it seems the cravings in one area die, I am compelled by the Holy Spirit to focus on another area.

My question becomes, "Can we control our cravings, and if so, how?" In a light way, I referenced this possibility in the opening remarks about my prior affections for soft drinks. It was a long way of making this point: Craving is directly tied to our consumption. Ultimately we crave whatever we are accustomed to consuming with regularity. When you drink soda consistently, your body yearns for soda. The same is true with our soul, spirit, and flesh life. Whatever we consume is what our soul will crave. If you reflect on the verses in 1 Peter 2, you will find that the encouragement to crave pure spiritual milk is a hidden commission to consistently consume spiritual things. Your internal cravings are directly connected to whatever it is you are routinely feeding your soul. If we make effort to adjust what we consume, and specifically if we focus on consuming things that are kingdom of God-oriented, our soul will eventually begin to crave increased spiritual activity.

A core point of journey in the Spirit-led life is to alter what the inner man craves. Obviously, the Holy Spirit is the One who changes us, but we hinder His role when we condition our soul to yearn for the accessories of this world instead. This begs us to ask deeper, more challenging questions.

Some may want to cover their eyes for a moment because we are going to wander into what some would call *legalism*. I find the concept of legalism and our proclivity to cry wolf concerning the label somewhat humorous and disingenuous. Simply stated, to consistently ask the question: "Is this permissible?" is to posture your heart in such a way that you will always test the boundaries located between the kingdom of God and the culture of the world. I assume that in reading this you have a heart to plunge more deeply into the waters of God. These are not questions about your entrance into the pearly gates or the condemning of your soul to hell. This is about Peter's invitation into the full experience of salvation. Maybe the more appropriate question to ask is about what is beneficial to a life of being in love with and receiving the love of God. Does this propel me toward freedom or continue to bog me down in my soul? What will aid in the removal of the filters distorting my view of Jesus and all He has accomplished on my behalf?

I am not talking about the removal of every "non-spiritual" activity from your life. I love sports. You have experiences you cherish as a part of the fabric of your life. I have been guilty, at various times in my life, of going on proverbial witch hunts, looking to burn anything not blatantly spiritual. I was no freer at the conclusion of the hunt than in the beginning. To the kingdom person, the lines between the sacred and the secular are less distinct and more blurred. A kingdom person finds value in the accessories of life that most miss. I am not an advocate of dividing your life into the categories of sacred and secular. However, I am an advocate for being sensitive enough to identify when we are feasting on something that pulls our heart nearer to the culture of heaven and when we are dining on something that pulls our heart deeper into a fallen state.

Do the activities I choose to do, the entertainment I enjoy, the relationships I have provoke legitimate or illegitimate cravings in my soul?

- Does this pull me toward greed or generosity?
- Does this pull me toward fear or security?
- Does this pull me toward lust or purity?
- Does this pull me toward sorrow or joy?
- Does this pull me toward angst or patience?
- Does this pull me toward anger or peace?
- What rises up in my soul when I participate in that activity, watch that show, listen to that station, or interact with that person?

Much of life just happens to us. We have so little control over many variables in our life—what happened to us as children, how someone treated us, the environment we were raised in, our health issues, the economic status of our first twenty years of life, and so on.

But we have complete control over what we consume on a daily basis. We may struggle with pain in our soul from an experience in our past, but why feed the pain? We may struggle with control issues because of some situation from our younger years that was out of our control, but why feed the control issues? To let our hearts go free is to, on some level, listen to what our hearts are trying to tell us about what we are consuming.

I know it is easier said than done, but get into what I call the "circle of life." The kingdom life, a life of freedom, works in a circular manner. You make a decision to consume well and this releases a kingdom benefit into your life. It releases joy or peace or hope or love. In turn, this release compels you to rightly consume again, which then again releases the supernatural into your life. Suddenly you find yourself in a circle of life.

In the opening pages of this book I made it clear that I do not presume to know the details of your life, nor do I have all the answers. However, I am confident Holy Spirit will give you wisdom and discernment. If you will learn to hear His voice, Holy Spirit is speaking to you. There have been times in my life in which I felt a "check" in my soul that I shouldn't watch, listen to, or participate in something. I would love to say I have always heeded the subtle nudge of Holy Spirit. I am learning the nudge is there more frequently than I once realized, and the more I honor it the more clearly I can identify its presence. That nudge always seems to come as I am moving toward something that could disturb my peace, joy, faith, hope, love, innocence, and confidence. Holy Spirit will help us seize control of our cravings if we will consistently respond appropriately to His interjections in the normal activity of our lives.

CHAPTER 11: THINK HIGHER

In my observations of church life and the common American believer, I have found that, by and large, we are very carnal in our thinking. Traditionally the word *carnal* carries a dark and evil connotation, but I reference it here in its more basic definition. Carnal means to be temporally minded, worldly, and humanistic in our thought patterns. My concern is that we are entirely too earthbound in our thinking. Peter has been a point of emphasis the last couple of chapters, so let's hear from him again.

> Dear friends, I warn you as "temporary residents and foreigners" to keep away from worldly desires that wage war against your very souls (1 Peter 2:11).

Peter is repeatedly reminding his readers about being heavenly minded.

If we objectively took stock of our daily happenings, customs, and habits, I fear we would find we are partakers of this world more than we would be comfortable admitting. If we read all of 1 Peter, an undercurrent is noticed. Peter's admonishment above was not only about sexual purity, lies, and depravity. As we read 1 Peter in its entirety, we discover that Peter is repeatedly reminding his readers about being heavenly minded. He refreshes their memory throughout the letter of an eternal dwelling awaiting them, and how all of life should be lived with this reality at the forefront. He cements those sentiments in stone with the statement that we are not really home here in this world. The common systems of operation surrounding us are not meant to be comfortable or familiar to us. Instead, they are cumbersome and feel like shackles. However, if one bears them as truth long enough, that which is foreign begins to feel like home. But this world and its ways are not our homeland. We are passing through. We are temporary renters tied to a culture that is far better.

> We become so now-minded that we lose sight of the utter contrast between the ideas of this world and those of heaven.

Yet all too often we become so now-minded that we lose sight of the utter contrast between the ideas of this world and those of heaven. We attach ourselves to worldly desires and principles and embrace them as truth. As previously stated, these worldly desires of which I speak are not necessarily sex and drugs. It could refer to a craving for power, the need to be in control, the yearning for creature comforts and the niceties of life, the sleepy lulling of entertainment, and the craving for acceptance and validation from the structure around us. It seems, in viewing the whole letter, that Peter was speaking of something in addition to sexual purity and the telling of the truth. He seems to be reminding us that our thoughts should be higher and not caught up in the pursuits of this life.

Let us again consider some difficult questions.

- Do I handle my finances in a worldly manner?
- Do I deal with people in a worldly way, routinely mindful of how they can benefit me?
- Do I lead my church or ministry based more on worldly concepts of business and success than I should?
- Do I view my occupation predominantly through the lens of paying bills and funding hobbies rather than through the lens of its benefit to God's kingdom and His glory?

I do not like those questions, but the heart becomes free when we are willing to give Holy Spirit access to probe a little deeper.

A few years ago I went on a mission trip to El Salvador. We worked with a wonderful ministry that especially emphasizes ministry to children. We stayed at their beautiful campground propped on the side of a mountain overlooking a lake that once was a volcano. Each morning we rose early to take a two-hour bus ride into the city. Along the way the scenery was stunning. Green mountains, smoldering volcanoes, fields of dried out lava rock—it was breathtaking. Then reality set in as we transitioned from the countryside to the city. You know the mission trip clichés. Their middle class housing would be considered condemnable here in the States. The streets were lined with what we call desperate poverty. We strolled down with our "right out of the mission trip handbook, straight from the rack of Bass Pro Shop" regalia. We entered schools and stood on sidewalks. We sang, we danced, we played soccer with the children, we dressed as clowns, and we preached—with an interpreter who may or may not have been able to translate our southern terminology.

In the midst of this, a young couple probably in their early thirties seemed to show up at every stop we made. After a couple of days, we realized they were a part of the church connected to the ministry we were there to serve. They did not speak English, but their love, generosity, and appreciation were more palpable than words. Oh, and their precious children. Their son was about the same age as my son. He was everything you would expect a four year old to be. Mischievousness, curiosity, and childlike wonder transcend national borders. Their daughter, not yet one year old, was adorable. The husband worked as a manager at a fast food restaurant in the city and his wife took care of the kids and served the ministry however she could. Their little family became favorites early in the week, and our affections for them were sealed when they invited us to their home during a break in ministry. They wanted to bless us. They wanted to honor us. They didn't look at us as the clueless outsiders that we, in reality, were. They saw us as family tied to one another by something deeper than cultural norms, last names, and DNA. We climbed off the bus, crossed a narrow street and entered their humble abode.

LET YOUR HEART GO FREE

In their home, one could sense the love of brotherhood and the presence of Jesus. We walked through their house as they handed us soda—yes, soda—haha. And I drank it with much joy because it was more than a beverage; it was an expression of generosity, hospitality, and brotherly love. Eventually, they ushered us to a small courtyard behind their house where they, through an interpreter, shared a little of their story with us. The neighboring house recently had come up for sale. Though the couple did not have the luxury of a surplus of expendable funds, they felt compelled by the Lord to purchase the house for the purpose of God's kingdom. It was their intention to convert the house into a place of prayer and as a version of a local church for their street. We all nodded in agreement, though we had yet to fully understand the gravity of this decision. The house had been vacant for some time. During its days of vacancy, the local gang used it as a hub. It had become a gang "clubhouse" of sorts. The wall of this vacant house was literally inches from the wall of the couple's home. When the gang members heard of the purchase of the house, naturally they were disgruntled. Their hangout was now under the ownership of a fast food restauranteur, a stay-at-home mom, and two precious children. To say they were not happy is an understatement.

I don't know how much you know about the culture of El Salvador. I was pretty ignorant of its history when I planned this trip for a bunch of teenagers. However, my eyes were opened when, a few months before the trip, I tried to get life insurance. I wasn't getting life insurance because of the trip. I was getting it as an act of caring for my wife and kids in general. When I applied for a life insurance policy, one of the questions they asked was, "Are you going out of the country any time in the next six months." My answer was a breezy, "Yes, I am going to El Salvador." We went through the remaining questions and my assumption, along with that of the customer service representative, was that in a few weeks I would be covered and I could check it off my to-do list. My assumption was inaccurate. A few weeks later, I received a call notifying me I had been denied in my application for life insurance because of my trip to El Salvador. The agent informed me El Salvador was considered one of the most dangerous nations in the world with a gang violence problem unrivaled anywhere.

This precious family was in the crosshairs of a collection of people who would not think twice about inflicting harm or kidnapping their children. These people were ruthless and quickly began to make threats. The couple explained to us how they were terrified for about three weeks after they purchased the neighboring house. They were extremely cautious and understandably wracked with fear. Then, one Sunday, they went to the altar and surrendered it all to the Lord. They had a breakthrough. The fear lifted and they determined in their hearts—get this—that if they died for the cause of Christ, then so be it. Their lives were not of greater worth than His kingdom. They made this decision fully aware of the ramifications it could have on their two precious children. Before you get cynical, this story was verified by several people connected to the church.

Our hearts swelled with compassion and admiration and a tidal wave of conviction. But the story doesn't end there. We returned to the bus and all agreed we needed to return the favor of hospitality and brotherly love, so we did the most American church thing we could think of: We passed a hat around the bus and collected an offering. We didn't make any speeches or give an offering sermon. We all simply agreed and started emptying pockets. One young man in particular came back later and gave a second time because he felt the Lord nudging him to give a specific amount. We counted the money and put it in an envelope, which we handed to the couple a few days later. To the best of our ability we conveyed our affection and admiration. We hoped the offering would say more than our broken Spanish could express. The next day, we did ministry at their church. After the service, they found me and once again, through an interpreter and tears, told another story about their life.

Two months prior to our visit to El Salvador, the husband received a bonus from his work. He and his wife agreed to use the bonus to make repairs on their car, pay off some debt, and purchase some very necessary items for their kids. This was a good, logical, and makes-all-the-sense-in-the-world plan. Then God intervened with a different, less logical, less reasonable plan. They were having dinner with a missionary to India who was visiting their church. While having dinner, Holy Spirit spoke to them about taking the bonus money and giving it to the missionary. Little discussion was needed. They heard the voice of God and immediately said yes. The next day, they went to the bank and took the bonus out of their account. Then they withdrew the rest of the money in their account. Yes, they zeroed out their checking and savings. They gave it *all* to the missionary. Once again, they understood this decision would affect not only them, but their children. Here I was, listening to this sweet couple pouring out their hearts, tears flooding their face and beginning to soak their shirts. You know where this story is going, don't you? In their hand was the white envelope containing the offering we gathered on the bus after we left their home. In the white envelope was the exact amount of money they had taken out of their bank account two months prior and given to the missionary to India. I want to jump up from my desk right now and run around the room celebrating what the Lord has done!

Here we sit, with our reason, logic, and practical living. Here we sit, stifling our faith by being enamored with a world and systems that cannot hold life.

> For my people have done two evil things: They have abandoned me—the fountain of living water. And they have dug for themselves cracked cisterns that can hold no water at all! (Jeremiah 2:13)

There is this glorious existence made available through Jesus, and we trade the living water for faulty operating systems that cannot hold anything of real value! In light of this experience, on the return flight, the questions flowed.

At times, we believers have tried very hard to appear normal in the eyes of other people. "Yes, I'm a Christian, but look how normal I am… please don't lump me into the category of weird, strange, or foolish." On some level we do it to try to salvage Jesus' reputation in the eyes of the world. Our thinking at times is, *If I can appear normal, the world won't judge Jesus so harshly and I can compensate for all the believers out there whom I perceive have misrepresented Him.* This is especially true in church leadership circles. We have embraced the ideology of looking more palatable to the world in hopes that they may embrace a gospel that is in complete contradiction to the ways of this world. It seems a little foolish when you phrase it that way. In the process, we dilute our true selves. We dilute our edge. We corrupt our craving.

This is not a commission to eliminate everything that lacks "eternal significance." It's more about remembering who we really are and where our true home is found. He is our home. He is our identity.

CHAPTER 12: BEACH BALL

These last few chapters have been a little heavy. I want to take a reprieve from that intensity for a few pages. The previous chapters have caused us to examine ourselves and ask difficult questions. In the midst of the asking, it is easy to be discouraged. It is easy to start taking on frustration or disappointment. Our frail imperfection seems to never cease to be on display. If you find yourself wrestling with Babel, cravings, a challenging set of personal history filters and geographical lenses, and you are wondering if you will ever know the "full salvation" Peter refers to in his letters, relax.

As I stated in the introduction, I've essentially been at this Christian thing my entire life. Unfortunately there are some aspects of the goodness and love of God that took me entirely too long to figure out. The majority of my days in Christ were spent trying really (I mean really) hard at pleasing the Father, yet ultimately always feeling like a disappointment. I read, "All fall short of the glory of God" (Romans 3:23) and perceived it as a challenge, rather than a statement of fact and an encouragement of how God's glory reaches down at our point of falling. I know what it is to wave my sword at the darkness, hoping to conquer the illegitimate desires in my heart. I was intimate with the effort of compiling as many spiritual disciplines and "good days" as I could muster so I could leverage them to pull myself out of the pit of disappointing God.

I have met many through the years who find themselves playing a secret game. They count days:

- How many days in a row they pray;

- How many days in a row they go without committing "that" sin;
- How many days in a row they read the Bible;
- How many days in a row they get it "right" instead of "messing up"; and so on.

The emotional and spiritual vibe of the person is heavily contingent on the count. The more good days accumulated, the better a person feels. Confidence is more easily accessible. Faith is high. Happiness is elevated. A sense of right standing with the Lord permeates. Worship is easier. Looking people in the eye requires less effort. It is amazing how stringing a succession of positive days together can affect the psyche.

> I have met many through the years who find themselves playing a secret game. They count days.

Going to the beach has always been something my wife and I enjoy. Having two kids in tow has certainly changed the dynamic, but we still load up our automobile routinely and make the drive to paradise. I recall days of leisure, sitting under the shade of an umbrella, lounging in a comfortable chair, toes in the sand, the sea breeze misting my face, the sound of waves crashing and a good book in my hand. Now that I'm a dad, the experience at the beach has changed ever so slightly. I transitioned from carefree relaxation to uptight anxiety as I watch my young children being overtaken by the tide. The waves, once tranquil, now have an air of death to them. It is amazing how as a parent the most common activity can morph into something deadly. I spend most of my time on the beach these days on the edge of my seat or in the water making sure the kids are safe. Don't get me wrong, I love having the kids with us at the beach, but occasionally I recall with fondness what it was like when it was just me and Michelle. In those days we had so much time available. With all of the excess time on our hands, we often found ourselves playing a game. It's one of the most addictive yet annoying games I have ever played. The odds are good you have participated in this recreation as well. We would stand facing each other, a few feet separating us. I would take a beach ball and hit it in the air toward Michelle. She would hit it back in my direction. With each strike of the ball we kept a running tabulation: 1...2...3...4...5...6...7...8...9...10. Eventually the ball would hit the ground. One of us would pick the ball up and resume the game: 1...2...3...4...5...6...7...8...9...55...63...75...89 and the ball would hit the ground. One of us would pick up the ball and resume the game: 1...2...3...4...5...6...7...8...9...24...46...68...88...115...

The larger the number, the more anxious and incredibly cautious the striking of the beach ball would become. I have watched countless believers play a similar game with their faith. I live with the ominous sense that eventually this ball is going to hit the ground and I will have to begin again at 1. Eventually I am going to mess up and I will have to start all over. Eventually I will miss a day of prayer, a day of Bible study. With each drop of the ball, much of the confidence we built, faith, happiness, sense of right standing with the Lord, and easy worship crashes to the ground. We go from lifting our heads high to hanging them in shame. Sure, we maintain an air of "got it togetherness" in front of others, but the inner man feels defeated, disappointed, and frustrated. It is exhausting to start over. It becomes a great discourager of our faith. Moving forward becomes pointless because it is inevitable that the ball will be dropped. And make no mistake: You will drop the ball again. So many followers of Jesus cease in following and simply exist within the realm of having a form of godliness without the power because of this. I know the feeling of despair, the guilt, the frustration with self that saturates every aspect of my mustered-up faith.

I believe Jesus plays the game differently than we do.

He certainly counts differently: 1...2...3...4...5...6...7...8...9...

The ball drops to the ground.

He looks your way, hoping to lock eyes, no disgust or annoyance in His countenance, no hint of disappointment.

He picks the ball back up and resumes the game: 10…11…12…13…14…15…16…17…18…

The ball drops to the ground. He nods to you to pick up the ball to resume the game: 19…20…21…22…23…24…25…26…

The ball drops, the game resumes from now until the end, *never returning to 1*.

Get this. Jesus never starts back at one! He doesn't put you in the cycle of performance where you have to get it perfect to progress further. He allows you to pick up the ball. He resumes counting and allows you to progress from the last drop of the ball!

> Jesus never starts back at one! He doesn't put you in the cycle of performance where you have to get it perfect to progress further.

Imagine how liberating it is to not live with the anxiety of the ball hitting the ground! I assure you—one mess up will not put Him back in the grave! Your bad day cannot override the greatest day in history. Your bad day does not have the same power as His glorious day. The cross and the empty grave are not robbed of their power by your sin. We have at times preached an impotent gospel, placing the power of Christ's finished work in submission to our capability to always get it right.

Admittedly, the majority of my journey with Jesus has been traveled within a theological echo chamber. I grew up in a Pentecostal environment, went to college in a Pentecostal environment, and have worked exclusively in that environment. To say I fit in the category of "Pentecostalism" is a safe statement. I would venture to say this is common for most of us, in that we trend toward surrounding ourselves with people of similar theology and like-mindedness. I don't necessarily believe this is a horrible practice; however, within most idea vacuums there are a few blind spots or, at the least, blurred spots. With that said, I may make a few stereotypical statements that are more or less a caricature (exaggerated interpretation of a reality) of the theological ideas of my Baptist brothers and sisters. I do so only to point out that my Pentecostal response to those caricatures through the years may have created some of the aforementioned blurred spots.

I grew up with the understanding there are two fundamental differences between "Baptist theology" and "Pentecostal theology." First, "we" talk in tongues and "they" don't believe in that. (I don't have time to address the unhealthy, ungodly "we" and "they" mentality to which we at times adhere). Second, they believe in the doctrine of the eternal security of the believer, a.k.a. "Once saved, always saved." I want to go on record that I remain firmly camped in the school of thought that a believer can indeed forfeit his or her redemption through willful disobedience and an unwillingness to say "yes" to Jesus. However, I am incredibly optimistic about the mercy of God and overwhelmingly confident in the love of God expressed through the person of Jesus. However, my observations through the years, along with the theological journey the Lord has had me on for quite some time now, leads me to the conclusion that the common retort of Pentecostalism to "Once saved, always saved" has caused the perpetuation of a paper thin gospel.

I fear that growing up as a Pentecostal, I frequently painted myself into a corner, diminishing the potency of the cross and the empty grave. We passionately celebrate the power of the cross to redeem the desperate sinner, all the while diminishing the glory of the empty grave's capability of keeping us in spite of our weakness. In our efforts to modify the behavior of believers and admonish the saints to a life of holiness, we routinely usurp the power of the gospel and put it in our own hands. For a good percentage of my life, sure the gospel was good news, but it was also stressful news. So much of the onus was on my ability to "live right"; thus, my gaze all too often left the splendor of Jesus and was fixed upon all my own deficiencies.

Don't misread this as a softening on holy, upright living. Instead, interpret it this way: The Father is not as fickle as we may have first believed. Jesus' efforts were strong and mighty. Holy Spirit operates in the fruit of patience with us as we are processed deeper into our faith. His love is strong and trustworthy. I have spent many years in my faith with the strain in my soul that my eternal hope was insecure and subject predominantly to my performance. The irony is that all the focus given to hold tightly to my salvation often made it difficult for me to receive grace. This pressure becomes a breeding ground for the expanding of our weaknesses, as the subtle uncertainty of God's love and the angst of disappointing the Lord feeds the flesh. The tighter I squeezed, the more my flesh gloried—not just in active sin but in pride, fear, ambition, and worry. I type today living with a deeper degree of consecration, a richer holiness, and an increased measure of the fruit of Holy Spirit—all because I have learned to rely on the power of the cross and resurrection as opposed to my own strength.

On Easter weekend around the world, we celebrate the oxymoronic beauty of the cross and the splendid victory of the rolled away stone. Let us not strip it of its glory in our fear that people will feel a license to do wrong. Fear and control are illegitimate catalysts. The wild, unceasing river of love of Jesus expressed on Calvary is the ultimate deterrent to sin and the most legitimate motivator to purity and rich faith.

So what happens when the ball drops? How do I respond? What do I do? By all means, I confess and ask for mercy and forgiveness. But we must also look Him in the face and trust His eyes of love! Our ability is undependable, but His love is a rock upon which all meaningful things are built. We don't hold our head in shame. We don't recoil from expressions of worship and faith as some form of twisted penance. We don't worry ourselves about "being a hypocrite." By the way, the word *hypocrite* is one of the most misused ideas in Christendom. It is typically used one of two ways—first as a justification to leave the faith because of "all of those hypocrite Christians." Second, it is often used as an instrument to control people when they aren't behaving the way we want them to behave. Hypocrisy has little to do with your bad day, your genuine struggle to overcome sin, or the audacity of lifting your hands in worship, even though you have had a less than stellar week (according to your performance). Hypocrisy is the accusation, by

Jesus, levied on the spiritual leaders who consciously used religious regulations to manipulate and control the people, all while dismissing those same regulations personally. Paul's version of hypocrisy was in regard to willful deceit of those around him. When we blow it, when we fall short of God's glory, we can trust His love. We pick up the ball and keep playing. He can handle it. He already has handled it.

Hey, listen closely. The odds are *very* high that you aren't a hypocrite. Quit counting days and start looking into love.

CHAPTER 13:
INCREMENTAL

Most of us examine our spiritual life through too broad of a lens. We look at what we want to be and then we look at what we are. We formulate a picture of what we want to look like, and in comparing that to who we are presently we become frustrated and disappointed. We think: *I'm not the person I should be.* We evaluate our spirituality in overtly black-and-white terms as either being "on fire" or not. Yes, I know the lukewarm will be vomited out of the mouth of God (Revelation 3:16), but your "following Jesus" life is very nuanced and not always easy to put into a specific category. What does "passionate" look like now versus when I was younger? What if God's definition of my walk with Him evolves as He processes me through experience and new revelation? Even with those questions creating unique layers to our spiritual life, I have found many believers are perpetually disappointed in themselves. How do we remedy this disease?

Often our response to this disappointment is to become "binge Christians." I'm sure you are familiar with binging as it relates to an eating disorder. A person eats a tremendous amount of food and then, ultimately, vomits the food out because their system cannot handle that volume. Obviously binging is an incredibly unhealthy means to maintain a desired weight. In the early phases, it erroneously helps a person manage their weight. The first season of binging is not catastrophic. However, over time the body corrodes. Vital organs become compromised to the extent that death can occur. The body cannot sustain the rhythm.

LET YOUR HEART GO FREE

Spiritually speaking, binging is equally dangerous. We go on runs of intense devotion and then we become angry with ourselves when we cannot maintain the pace. We don't necessarily slip into sin patterns, but we do slip into seasons of lackluster, guilt-ridden engagement. Listen, we can spend our time with our head in utopian clouds or we can speak candidly about where most of us live spiritually. We often read the Bible and extract some of the wrong ideas. We flip from glorious account to glorious account of the heroes of the faith. We read of Elijah calling fire down from heaven, Moses at the edge of the Red Sea, and Paul performing extraordinary feats. I am in no way saying the Bible is flawed. However, within its pages we are not often privileged with the opportunity to see the "everyday" of the men and women of faith. We get snapshots of their highlights and at times their moments of failure. But the consistent rising in the morning and lying down of the evening are absent from the pages, understandably so. The Bible was never meant to be a collection of stories, pointing out heroes to be emulated. The accounts of men and women in Scripture are not meant to be bars raised to a height that we are expected to emulate. It is a book of Jesus. It is about the heart of the Father. It is about the activity of Holy Spirit. To dismiss the mundane of life, the seemingly inconsequential days, is to set ourselves up for grave disappointment and a strong sense of failure. We look at Mount Carmel (1 Kings 18) with the fire from heaven and become disillusioned because we don't live there ourselves. Neither did Elijah. We esteem the idea of spiritual maturity too often through the lens of extraordinary feats rather than the lens of simple consistency. Maturity and freedom in the life of faith are less about grand gestures and more about elementary devotion.

> Maturity and freedom in the life of faith are less about grand gestures and more about elementary devotion.

All too often, our response is to identify an area of our life that is inconsistent or weak and start barraging it for a season.

- "Let me fix this problem I have identified."
- "I'm going to change my schedule."
- "I'm going to get up at the crack of dawn."
- "I'm going to shut off my computer or satellite."

The barrage, for a short season, works for us. Yet over time, the barrage becomes unsustainable with our everyday existence, and we eventually return to our more common patterns.

- "I'm going to wake up two hours earlier each day to pray."
- "I'm going to fast lunch every day from here until Jesus comes back."
- "I'm going to read the entire New Testament in a month."

At first, we have great energy and genuine dedication. Yet at some point, we find our way back to the well-worn paths of our life. We default to the systems that have been most frequently applied throughout our life. It is too difficult to live in the barrage. It isn't sustainable.

The truth is we are lacking in the necessary strength to change most of what is wrong with us.

The more appropriate approach is to consistently engage God with purpose and allow Him to refine those areas. For many believers in Jesus, a massive overhaul is not what is needed. Rather, it is slight adjustments to perspective, schedule, thinking, and so on, which over an extended time frame results in what appears to be dramatic change. The truth is we are lacking in the necessary strength to change most of what is wrong with us. We need the supernatural power of God to overcome our flesh. Therefore, we must find a rhythm in which the Holy Spirit has room to operate. A pastor friend of mine, Eddie Turner, stated it this way: "The Holy Spirit flows. Therefore, for the supernatural of God to flow in one's life a rhythm must be established."

LET YOUR HEART GO FREE

In recent years, I started going to the gym. This isn't my first round of physical fitness efforts. If you saw me at the beach, you would probably have doubts I have ever seen a dumbbell. However, through trial and error, I have learned some lessons about exercise and fitness. One lesson learned (and it is the same with dieting) is that one does not "get ripped" or fix "problem areas" adequately with short bursts of frenetic energy. And if you happen to do so, most often the rhythm is unsustainable. Therefore, you temporarily "fix" the problem, but it will ultimately return because you could not maintain the lifestyle that led to the improvements. When my son was first born, I spent a season working from a home office. To be completely honest, I spent substantially more time parenting than working on my job, but it was worth it. Because I was at home a good part of the day, I decided to try out one of the latest workout fads. I didn't buy the DVD collection because I wasn't so serious that I wanted to drop money on the table. However, I did have a friend who loaned me his DVD set. I started the program and did my best to maintain the regimen. Because of the liberty I had in my schedule, I was able to devote the required 1.5 hours a day necessary to get the desired results. I put my son in his high chair, and kept the snacks and TV rolling. I'm sure some super parent out there is groaning. At the conclusion of the program I did not look like the guy on the video, but I did feel more physically fit and looked better than I had ever thought possible.

The problem is that life happens, jobs change, and the intense pace of the workout program became impossible to maintain. What happened? I resumed old habits and lost whatever progress I had made during the "binge." Fast forward to this season of my life. Based upon my responsibilities on all fronts, the idea of giving 1.5 hours a day to exercise is no longer realistic. It is unsustainable. Therefore, I have had to make adjustments. I've had to become more realistic in my approach. I have determined that a consistent, sustainable approach over time will develop within me a pattern of being fit. The same applies spiritually. If we are being honest, the binge workout to "get ripped" is touched with a measure of vanity and pride. The incremental approach of being healthy is touched with wisdom and perspective. I wonder, in my life, if my binge spiritual efforts were often more driven by the pride and vanity of being perceived as spiritual rather than a sincere seeking of the Lord. This is a question I am asking myself—one maybe we should all ask ourselves. A life focused on incremental progress is one of wisdom, disregarding the outside observation of others and concerning itself instead with the only legitimate audience: Jesus. The process becomes of far greater value than the result, and this is an incredible kingdom culture principle.

> *"My responsibility is not improvement. My responsibility is engagement."*

In our spiritual life we must resist the thought process of "fixing ourselves" in one fell swoop. I believe in "suddenlies"; I believe God can, in a moment, dramatically alter one's life. I have witnessed miracles, healings, divine provision, and instant change. However, more often than not, we are in process. The process has a different pace during different seasons of our life. As difficult as this is to embrace, I have to understand there are dynamics in my life that may not be completely meshed with the ways of God's kingdom by the end of the year. There are some areas God may process for the next five years or more, peeling back layer upon layer. Am I OK with this? I choose to be OK with it because, regardless of how much you lean toward Calvinism or Arminianism, we all must accept the fact that God does things in His timing, not ours.

Please don't attempt to read too much into this. I am not diminishing the necessity and value of passion. I place a high value on passion, especially that which is pointed toward the Lord. Even so, throughout my life I have grown frustrated with seasonal passion—stretches of life marked with high levels of passion followed by stretches in which it is a challenge to muster up any passion. I have discovered that incremental consistency leads to a more authentic public passion. A more authentic passion that is not laced with a tinge of guilt because we can recall our former eras of deficient passion.

I preach. I have, for years, stood on platforms wielding a microphone. Truth be told, I have become quite skilled at appearing passionate. Even in those seasons of my life in which I was not manifesting passion off the platform. This has occurred more frequently than I care to admit. And for the person who has a conscience, it's a miserable existence. I've had many "come to Jesus" moments in which I wondered if I was fraudulent. Yet there is a distinct difference between being a fraud and being flawed. As we discussed before, my guess is that you are not a hypocrite. However, this does not diminish the legitimate strain created in our soul when we feign public passion, knowing our private experience is lackluster. My hope for us all is that we would manifest a legitimate passion, derived not from the necessity of the moment but from the well we have dug through consistent, everyday moments.

There is a distinct difference between being a fraud and being flawed.

To what do we need to apply a consistent, incremental thought process? Here is where you check your brain out for a moment if you are a long-time Christian because you've heard this list countless times: We pray. We read the Bible. We worship. We fast. We meditate. We give thanks. We listen to His voice. We spend time in Jesus' presence. One of my greatest deterrents to those disciplines (yes, disciplines) is my unrealistic expectation of the immediate results. Every one of us wants a prayer life that feels as if we have poked our head through the clouds and are in heavenly places. We want a Scripture life full of fresh, new revelation that blows our ever-loving minds. We want our moments of worship and thanksgiving to be met with a rushing wind and a cloud of glory. We want it all to be incredibly glorious! Then we carve out a niche in our day, shut out the world, reach toward the heavens...and there are no fireworks...no glory cloud...no supernatural visions. After that, you go hear someone preach and they begin to tell of their latest divine interruption and they make it sound like God is a chatterbox in their life. And here we are, left wondering what is wrong with us. Am I doing it wrong? Is there some formula? Maybe if I spend more minutes it will get better?

We must dismiss goals when we pray or read. Praying and reading **are** the goal.

My life experiences are possibly different from yours. I have grown up in a fellowship that places a high value on the activity of Holy Spirit and the experience of God's presence. I have had tremendous encounters with God—so formative that to this day I don't think I can adequately articulate what happened. But there has been a vast number of days in between that don't appear especially spectacular. For years I carried a guilt that I wasn't doing enough and a fear that God was not fully pleased. And then, things started to change. Do you want to know what changed? It wasn't more hours or better scheduling. I came to a startlingly simple truth. Entering prayer with a goal, even the noble goal of encountering God's presence, was detrimental to my attempt at spiritual disciplines. *We must dismiss goals when we pray or read. Praying and reading are the goal.* Extending myself toward my Father is the goal. Opening my soul to commune with Him is the goal. I stopped entering prayer, study, worship, and meditation with the pressure that something "had to happen." I quit having expectations. For a guy like me, this remains counterintuitive. I have come up in a culture in which expectancy is vital as it relates to God engaging His people.

I was taught the following:

"If you come expecting, God will meet you."

"There is so much expectancy in this room that we know God will show up."

Once again, don't read beyond the words or try to read my mind. I place a premium on coming together as a people with great anticipation of

God hearing our cry and moving among us. I witness the manifestation of God's goodness in corporate settings on a regular basis. That manifestation, in my experience, is often directly correlated to the expectation of the people revealed in their worship and response to God. On many occasions I have been in the room as miracles occurred and the glory of God was evident. However, in my personal life, I began to realize that placing those expectations on my everyday disciplines served more as a deterrent than a catalyst. As a pleasant surprise, I have found visitations of God's presence are more frequent and consistent as I diminish the straining and striving that is often attached to the pressure.

The goal, the one expectation we should have of ourselves, is to become consistent in our engagement of God. Prayer, study, meditation, thanksgiving are not in pursuit of God's glory. Rather, God's glory is in pursuit of those who are consistent in their approach. To borrow a pattern from the Old Testament: David accumulated the materials and Solomon saw the temple built to completion. Once the structure was in place, God's glory came and filled the temple. It is probably another book for another day, but it is a healthy thought process to understand this:

"You don't find God's glory. God's glory finds you."

And the more you are consistently available, the more frequently you will experience this wonderful finding. The freedom your heart longs for is occasionally attached to a grand moment of divine interaction. However, more often it is in conjunction with the simplicity of showing up repeatedly with little fanfare. Every day of prayer and study is not straight glory, but I am amazed at how many times He breaks into my simple, sustainable approach. However, on the days you do not feel much at all, you can rest assured that the mere effort of opening your soul to interact with the divine One will lead to an incremental altering of who you are. Open up your ancient gates that the King of Glory may come in (Psalm 24)—some days with intensity and some days almost completely unnoticeable. Nonetheless, He comes.

CHAPTER 14: TIME(S) MANAGEMENT

As previously stated, I preach. One of the great challenges of preaching is the sense of obligation to be fixed on a particular end result for one's message—especially in the Spirit-filled / Pentecostal / Charismatic (you pick whichever label you prefer) circles with which I am familiar. We preach to an end. However, the beauty of a book is the relief of putting a series of thoughts out for public consumption and trusting Holy Spirit and the reader enough that they will discuss it with one another as they move forward. It is unlikely I will see the result in your life, and I am content within this reality. I am relatively comfortable with things that are ambiguous and open-ended. At this point you have probably discerned that it would be inaccurate to label me as rigid. It would also be feasible to say I am not a regimented, highly disciplined personality type. On the surface this may seem to disqualify me from discussing a thought like time management, but I think quite opposite. I have encountered countless lovers of God who felt inept in how they managed their time. With this sense of ineptitude comes a landslide of guilt, remorse, insecurity, and shame. Once again, I do not intend to offer a license for sloth, but I do think I understand that the struggle is real. I am not a guru on a leadership mountaintop, talking down to the peasants who just cannot get it right. I am with you in this tension. I have felt the condescension from leaders extraordinaire and have borne the sting of "not enough."

For me, language matters. Adding specific language to different arenas of my life has empowered me in the place of prayer as well as in my focus. Maybe language doesn't work the same for you, but in my life time management has been greatly assisted by giving specific designations.

With that being said, here are two words that will give us some borders through the next few pages.

Chronos

This is a Greek word referring to chronological or sequential time. *Chronos* alludes to the ticking of the clock, the twenty-four-hour increments of life. It is our everyday existence on the calendar.[7] It is quantitative. It is measurable and tangible. It is ever-present and unceasing in its flow. It moves and has a specific, repetitive allotment within each rotation of the earth on its axis and on every trip this planet makes around the sun.

On the other hand, there is…

Kairos

While *chronos* is quantitative, *kairos* is qualitative, which means it is measured by quality rather than quantity.[8] *Kairos*, in the ancient Greek, means "season." It is a word with a loose connection to weather, which indicates an ebb and flow. Whereas *chronos* is never disrupted, *kairos* has a readability requiring perception. People like Aristotle, a pagan of sorts, viewed the word *kairos* as a passing instant when an opening appears. *Kairos* in Aristotle's era was about being able to recognize the possibilities of a moment in time and having the ability to adapt to the moment. In New Testament terminology, which holds more bearing to us, *kairos* was used approximately eighty times and is perceived as "the appointed time in the purpose of God."

Kairos is the glory. *Chronos* is the grind.

I liken *kairos* to the "God moments" of life—the open windows of heaven, the "seasons of promotion." *Kairos* is the glory. *Chronos* is the grind. I certainly love the *kairos* of life—those pockets within the

---

7. James Strong, "Strong's Greek: 5550. χρόνος (chronos) -- Time," accessed May 05, 2018, http://biblehub.com/str/greek/5550.htm.

8. James Strong, "Strong's Greek: 2540. καιρός (kairos) -- Time, Season," accessed May 05, 2018, http://biblehub.com/greek/2540.htm.

framework of time that seem to defy normalcy and find us positioned under what seems to be a portal from heaven. Those stretches of life that feel as if we are staring at Jacob's ladder (Genesis 28), witnessing the ascending and descending of angels from heavenly realms into this earthly domain. Your mind is now being pulled back to some particular era in your life in which you recall the sweetness of God's fragrance permeating your life. I certainly reminisce about those moments and eagerly anticipate the next time my *chronos* intersects with the world-defying expressions of heaven. Despite the glorious joy of finding oneself in a *kairos* moment, our reality says a large percentage of our life is spent in the ticking clock of day-to-day existence.

It is of great importance that we become astute at discerning the nature, duration, and intent of *kairos* moments. The writer of Ecclesiastes (we assume Solomon) expressed the necessity of deciphering the times.

For everything there is a season, a time for every activity under heaven.
A time to be born and a time to die.
A time to plant and a time to harvest.
A time to kill and a time to heal.
A time to tear down and a time to build up.
A time to cry and a time to laugh.
A time to grieve and a time to dance.
A time to scatter stones and a time to gather stones.
A time to embrace and a time to turn away.
A time to search and a time to quit searching.
A time to keep and a time to throw away.
A time to tear and a time to mend.
A time to be quiet and a time to speak.
A time to love and a time to hate.
A time for war and a time for peace (Ecclesiastes 3:1-8).

It seems the writer wanted to clearly paint a picture that one must be perceptive when it comes to time. This was a beautiful moment in literature, which has been quoted by those with little God consciousness. However, Solomon expressed these thoughts not from a humanistic or philosophical perspective, but from the vacuum of God. By this I mean, none of those times were meant to be weighed and pondered outside of the wisdom of God. More importantly, Solomon wanted to capture the attention of the reader and hone in on a life necessity. We must have a sensitivity to us, a sixth sense of sorts, enabling us to rightly divine what is happening around us as it relates to *chronos* and *kairos*. For us all, there is a desire to be so in tune with the heart of heaven that we clearly distinguish those appointed times in the purpose of God. However, I have come to a stark reality in my life. The *kairos*, our ability to perceive and receive it, is intrinsically bound to our management of the *chronos* of life. The flow of your *chronos* affects your ability to perceive and have proper perspective regarding the *kairos*. The inverse is true as well. Our perspective and perception of the *kairos* gives weight to, or diminishes, the significance of our *chronos*. It is difficult to find value and fulfillment in our everyday existence if we are not highly sensitive to what the Lord is doing in the bigger picture of life. Our God-consciousness makes the mundane rich. Our awareness of God in all things nullifies the concept of mundane altogether. The ability to receive Jesus from the common of our *chronos* enlivens even the rudimentary activity of life. I have found this to be true: If the every days are cumbersome or filled with detachment, it is easy to miss or misidentify what the Lord is doing in our present season. On the other hand, perceiving *kairos* is often most hindered by busyness in the *chronos*. As you see, the value of each dimension of "time" is linked intimately with the other.

> The ability to receive Jesus from the common of our *chronos* enlivens even the rudimentary activity of life.

Allow me to pause for a moment and make a balancing statement you can hold on to before we move ahead. I believe working hard is a biblical trait of a follower of Jesus. I believe integrity compels us to give our best efforts and refrain from a life of sloth. As the revelation of God is enlarged in our lives, we begin to view our labors from a different angle. The American philosophy behind hard work is that it enables personal advancement. This is a somewhat noble motivator for good work ethic. However, for the believer we have a deeper and more profound motivator:

It's all worship.

I work hard, not necessarily for a particular end result but because so much has been afforded to me through the cross and by my Father that anything less than my best unto Him seems sinful. Our motivator to put in the extra hours or go the extra mile or pay great attention to the seemingly insignificant details is not necessarily the pay raise or the public affirmation of a job well done. We are motivated by love, which is infinitely more forceful than personal progress or material gain. I make this balancing statement because over the next few pages we are going to examine the "flow" of our life and I do not want it to be misrepresented as offering a license for laziness. Rather, we are searching for any and everything that could possibly pave the way for a greater flow of Holy Spirit in our lives. Like much of this book (and all books in general), we must rely on the Holy Spirit for answers for our life because what works for the author of some book may not fit the unique existence carved out for you by the Father.

CHAPTER 15: RHYTHM

I t is my assumption, because you are investing the time to read this writing, that you have aspirations as a lover of God to be in sync with Holy Spirit. Flow and rhythm are directly linked to the manifestation of God's goodness and our effectiveness in His purposes.

> *"Holy Spirit flows, so it is vital you establish a rhythm to life, which facilitates the flow."*

For some this may mean a decrease in "busyness," but for others it may require a little more "busyness" and a little less lethargy. Simply stated, if our life doesn't have rhythm, the flow of the Holy Spirit is hindered. If we lack appropriate pace and space, it is inevitable that we will mismanage our *chronos* and be numb to the *kairos*.

The following is a working definition we will maintain as a reference point.

Rhythm is consistent pace and persistent routine.

Once upon a time I was a staff pastor in the local church. Many of you can identify with what I am about to share. The metallic-looking plastic plate on my incredibly cramped office door read "Youth Pastor." This was only because the shiny plastic was not large enough to also read outreach pastor, Sunday School teacher, occasional custodian, whatever is needed in the moment, and worship leader. On Wednesday nights I was in the youth room / fellowship hall / kids' ministry room / random place to put the organ we never use but don't want to get rid of because it would make *that* family angry room. I led students. However, on Sundays there I was in "big church"—microphone in hand, surrounded by an assortment of musicians leading worship. I genuinely enjoyed this facet of my role, but to say I was a musician would have been a fabrication. I sang, sometimes on key, and led the team. Despite my less-than-musical ability, I've had the joy through the years of becoming friends with some incredibly gifted and anointed musicians and psalmists. Any musician will tell you rhythm is *the* essential ingredient in all music.

Rhythm is derived from the Greek word *rhythmos,* which means any regular motion with symmetry.[9] It generally relates to movement marked by strong and weak elements. Rhythm implies moments of strength combined with moments of weakness. This rendering of the word can be traced deeper to another Greek word, *rhein,* which means flow or stream.[10] You have likely heard of the Rhine River in Europe. Regarding music, one can make sounds and play notes with beautiful instruments, but if there is no underlying "flow" then you are not making music. You are just making noise. Conversely, you can take non-instruments that make sound and create a sense of music if the sounds are tethered together by rhythm.

The earth was established with pace and rhythms.

Think about God and His splendid creation for a moment. The earth was established with pace and rhythms. It would be irresponsible for us to dismiss the nature of creation. I am firmly in the camp who believes in sporadic, miraculous happenings from the hand of God fueled by the faith of people. Yet, so much of what happens around us was set into motion at the beginning of all things by His voice. He seemingly allows it to flow since inception.

9. "Definition of Rhythmos," Definition of Rhythmos, Rhythmus (noun, LNS, Rhythmos, Rhythmus) - Numen - The Latin Lexicon - An Online Latin Dictionary, accessed May 04, 2018, http://latinlexicon.org/definition.php?p1=2051639.

10. "Rheo- and rhein," Dictionary.com, accessed May 04, 2018, http://www.dictionary.com/browse/rheo-.

Consider the following:

- The rhythmic moving of the ocean, consistently and repetitively drawing water out and then crashing back onto the shore.

- The cadence of a heartbeat that begins not long after conception and remains until the end of its days.

- The dependability of the Earth's rotation, which brings us the stillness of dawn and the peace of dusk.

Without realizing it, much of what we do in life eventually falls into a unique rhythm. You and I walk with a particular gait. Our speech often has a rather consistent cadence. Even menial tasks, like washing dishes or mowing the lawn, over time become so ingrained that, without conscious decision, we do them the same way repeatedly. God likes rhythm. He established numerous perpetual rhythms throughout creation. The truth is, your body, soul, and spirit crave rhythm as well. Everything works better when in rhythm.

From a worship leader's perspective, an occasional missed note is barely noticed and certainly does not derail the moment. A vocalist off key does not bring things to a halt. (Because the sound guy can just turn their microphone down, right sound technicians?) But if the rhythm is disrupted, every facet of the team begins to fall apart. This is why musicians who have honed their skill eventually find their way to a metronome, which assists in establishing rhythm as second nature. If you have ever been in a moment of music with a drummer who has no rhythm...well, you might as well just shut the thing down.

The problem with rhythm and flow is that they are dynamics requiring the opposite of what you would expect. We all have mental pictures and scenes attached to words. You hear words like *rhythm* and *flow* and they elicit thoughts of fields of flowers, dangling your toes in the river, and living a laid-back life. Therein lies the problem. Rhythm necessitates some measure of concrete discipline. I tend to perceive my relationship with God in more abstract terms because so much of Him leaves me with inadequate answers. He mesmerizes me with His ability to wholly be two things that are seemingly contradictory on the surface. He is a mystery that is never fully discovered. He can, to an unfathomable measure, be both a Judge and a Dispenser of boundless mercy. He can blaze with holy anger yet be ultimately defined as love. I have failed to successfully box Him into a convenient package, so my exploration of Him has become less dependent upon compartments. However, my abstract exploration of God requires a rhythm. It is a bit of an oxymoron, but to have flow I need some structure. A river operates no differently, for it requires parameters in order to have its full capacity of force and flow.

Growing up, I occasionally went fishing with my dad on a lake here in Tennessee ironically named Kentucky Lake. We now live in a new era in which technology has increased our information exponentially. But years ago, prior to the convenience of a GPS, things were not as exact. Kentucky Lake is massive in size. It is miles of water. Yet within the lake, there are rivers running freely. You can't really see them, but they have current and are often hotspots teeming with fish life. To the natural eye, the rivers are almost impossible to perceive because they are in the middle of a lake and they have no borders. Occasionally you would happen to drift across the flow of the river and notice the current there, but for the most part you were somewhat guessing at its whereabouts. In some spots there were buoys, noting its borders. Of course, the more frequently you fished the area, the more familiar you became with the currents within it. However, it was nothing like having a clear-cut, flowing river with banks. Those rivers with banks are easily noticed, perceived, and identified as such.

I liken the life of Holy Spirit to a river, which is not a stretch because the Bible also makes similar correlations. I want to be in tune to the degree that I can identify the activity of Holy Spirit and perceive His intentions. I desire a life highly sensitive to the ebb and flow of Holy Spirit, for that life has force beyond my ability and is teeming with glorious life. Yet often, I have felt like I did those days in a boat on Kentucky Lake. I knew the "river" was around and I occasionally crossed its path, but I did not have a mode of operating instituted in my life that enabled me to consistently find and perceive the river. Insufficient rhythm in my *chronos* makes the *kairos* seem random and elusive. Those moments I crossed His path almost seemed happenstance. A life marked by rhythm has better enabled me to notice, perceive, and identify the activity (flow) of Holy Spirit in, through, and around me. The borders, the banks, the concrete discipline, the rhythm gives me a keener ability to commune and connect with Holy Spirit. When the rhythm is in place, my awareness of God increases. When that rhythm is disrupted for extended periods of time, I sense a subtle numbness creeping into my soul.

I believe most everyone reading this book understands the need for personal discipline and some form of rhythm. I have known all my life that I needed to pray, read my Bible, manage my time well, and so on and so forth. The struggle is transitioning from intellectual information to actually creating the cadence. I cannot speak from a place of having completely conquered my *chronos,* but if you will allow I can share some "triggers" that have helped me establish rhythm. To be clear, I have said nothing about being regimented or hyper-disciplined. I do not wish to paint an inaccurate portrait of myself. What has aided me tremendously is the practice of creating a few stimulants that help me maintain rhythm. Notice I didn't say "daily" rhythm. I omitted "daily" intentionally. Some days are not like the others. Some days carry unique demands. These stimulants are meant to shift me back into rhythm when things get a little off. I think of them as a spiritual pacemaker. When the rhythm of a heart gets out of sequence, a subtle jolt by the pacemaker puts it back on pace. Rhythm, for me, is not a stringently planned schedule each day. It is not a minute-by-minute account of my activity. Rather, it is a matter of a consistent and persistent pattern over a duration of time.

If you don't mind me being a little personal for a moment, my triggers or stimulants come in the form of an alarm clock waking me before my wife and two kids. It is the cup of coffee as I sit in the same spot on the couch in my living room and read / journal a few verses of the Bible. It is the conversation with the Lord in the quiet about whatever is pressing on my heart. Then it is about the seven-minute drive to the local gym for a brief workout. In case your eyes just rolled, I have no delusions that my 6-foot 3-inch 155-pound frame will ever be herculean. I go to the gym not so much out of vanity or health as much as a means to jump-start my day and to hold me accountable to rhythm. I come home, get ready for work, drop my son off at school, and head to the office. On my desk is a Bible, always open. It is my desk Bible. It is a collection of paper detached from the cover. It never leaves my desk. I pick up where I left off the last time I sat at my desk and spend a few minutes journaling whatever I feel the Spirit of the Lord is saying about what I read. From there I start my job. I have a list—not an hour-to-hour list. It is a list of all I need to do over an extended period of time (usually a couple of months). I keep worship music playing in the background almost nonstop. Occasionally I will set multiple alarms on my phone to sound out through the day, calling my attention as a reminder to consider the Lord. I attempt to talk to Jesus throughout the day, keeping a running discourse with Him. At some point I go home and wrestle with the kids, eat dinner, and get ready for bed. For a few moments my kids lie in bed with me and I read them a passage of Scripture, tell them a Bible story, or preach a kid version of one of my sermons. I lie in bed with them, pray with them, prophetically declare over their lives, and kiss them good night.

Having read that, some of you may be distinctly unimpressed. Maybe you feel the need to read the book of someone who labors in the place of prayer for 2.5 hours before the rooster crows and never eats lunch because they are always fasting. For some reason I have all too often felt the intense desire to live vicariously through someone whom I presumed to be at a personally unattainable place of spiritual expression and discipline. I feel no need to defend myself, but I will say the expressions and depth of the rhythm vary from day to day and even have some stretches that seem unusually more "third heaven-like" and divine than other stretches. The point is that *kairos*, presence-of-God living requires some semblance of consistency and persistency. Each person has to find his or her rhythm. If you are hungry for Jesus, you look for opportunity to plunge more deeply. If you are an adherent to stale religion, you likely search out opportunities to validate a lack of pursuit.

To be honest, that is not every day of my life. Sometimes I travel for ministry. Some stretches of the year are hectic as the responsibilities of my job are heightened. Saturdays I sleep in. There are deviations from the routine mentioned above. Some days I live the rhythm to a tee and other days I do very little of what I mentioned. However, it is the pattern I can return to and it shifts me right back into sync. If things start feeling numb or off, I examine and often find the rhythm has been disrupted for an extended period of time. I have been amazed at how many times just a couple days of reapplying the "stimulants" reopens my soul and spirit. Your rhythm will likely look different from my rhythm. You have to identify and implement the stimulants that fit who you are and your pace of life. Whatever those may be, you need to establish something consistent and persistent. It may take on varying degrees of intensity during different *chronos* and *kairos* seasons of life, and that is fine. You may discover new rhythm during different seasons of life and that's fine as well. The point is, whatever the makeup of your life (occupation, parenthood, health, and so on), if there is not consistent repetition, you don't have rhythm.

For years I struggled with this because I get bored easily, find monotony to be soul crushing, and have been fascinated with the Big Picture of the *kairos* of life. For years I found it difficult to establish and maintain rhythm in my life. I had the all-too-familiar peaks and valleys in my faith. So what changed? As cliché as it may sound, everything shifted for me when my thinking changed. Follow me to the next chapter.

CHAPTER 16: PAGAN PRAYERS

What if I told you that the bulk of my prayer life through the years looked more like that of a pagan than a Christian? Make no mistake, I faithfully sealed most every prayer with "in Jesus' name," and I even quoted Scripture with regularity. You might assume by *pagan* that I mean I prayed selfish prayers or prayers for worldly things like money and possessions. Not accurate. I have always known selfishness is not godly and the love of money is the root of evil. What I call pagan prayer describes the internal posture and subtle motivation of why we pray.

I discovered along the way, with much help from Holy Spirit, that one of the greatest deterrents to managing my *chronos* and establishing rhythm was my thinking as I entered the place of prayer. My prayer life started with an almost insurmountable deficit, destined to discourage me from ever sufficiently engaging God with regularity. As is so often the case for us, my thinking paralyzed me. My thought processes were a bit in the horse's mouth, dictating and bridling the true desires of my wild heart. Paul says it this way in Romans:

> Don't copy the behavior and customs of this world, but let God transform you into a new person by changing the way you think. Then you will learn to know God's will for you, which is good and pleasing and perfect (Romans 12:2).

When our thinking changes, our life changes. For me, the thought change was dramatic. I stopped thinking about spiritual disciplines, productivity, holiness, and rhythm in the terms of:

- I don't want to disappoint God.

- I need to do more to gain His favor.

- I need to do more to increase the anointing on my life.

- I want to avoid the disapproval of God.

- I don't want God to be frustrated with me because I'm not praying or reading my Bible.

I can't remember the moment or the circumstances that led to this epiphany, but upon heartfelt examination and with the help of Holy Spirit I became aware that most of my relationship with my Father was rooted in fear and insecurity. The odds are high that many reading this have seen those same phrases waft across their consciousness. Sure, we intellectually understand this negative perspective is not quite accurate, but it is a very difficult mental bondage to break. I subversively and almost unconsciously assumed the Father's posture toward me was one of cynicism. I could not shake the nagging sensation of never being enough. I envisioned an annoyed God.

While there is not enough time to break down the pagan religions common in the Bible, the imagery is likely in your mind. The worshipers of Baal on Mt. Carmel cutting themselves and exhausting themselves to invoke their deity, the overt attempts to appease a god of harvest to ensure good crops, the excessive rituals to satiate a god of rain in a season of drought, the unorthodox maneuvering to soothe a clearly disappointed goddess during a rampant plague. To be a pagan was to live with an unrelenting sense of angst, insecurity, and fear; due to the underlying structure of the religion, the god they served was always on the precipice of dissatisfaction with its worshipers.

So I prayed like a pagan.

While I am reluctant to place percentages on it, I feel comfortable saying much of my life of prayer through the years was from a deficit. I started in the red. I opened behind. I prayed as if I had given up ten runs in the first inning of game seven in the World Series. I carried this inescapable sense of God being frustrated with me due to my vast array of deficiencies. I approached the Lord not from a posture of love, hope, and possibility but from fear, obligation, and appeasement instead. I entered His presence not so much boldly and with confidence, but with a sense of heaviness and a head held low.

> This undercurrent fear of disappointing God drives us to an impossible pursuit of perfection instead of a pursuit of the Perfect One.

The impetus of illegitimate "religion" is the unshakable sense that God is easily and consistently disappointed. This undercurrent fear of disappointing God drives us to an impossible pursuit of perfection instead of a pursuit of the Perfect One. Thus we become entangled in the web of the "systems" of Christianity rather than being intertwined with the person of Christ. As a result, even positive spiritual disciplines are diminished in value and difficult to maintain with any sense of rhythm because they are laced with the fear of meeting God's disapproval. Pagan culture carried out its religious disciplines in an effort to control and appease impossible-to-please gods. It is safe to say that much of my Christian life was more pagan in nature because its roots grew down into fear rather than love.

Ask yourself this challenging question and be honest in your searching:

- Is my faith based more on fear or love?
- Do I wrestle in my inner dialogue with anxiety over how well received I am by my Father in heaven?
- When I settle my soul to consider God, do I lead with the confidence of one loved, or with the timidity of one who is not quite certain if they are loved?

Of course, you intellectually know you are loved. If you were around church much as a kid, you had this fact drilled into your mind through the childhood tune, "Jesus loves me this I know, for the Bible tells me so."

LET YOUR HEART GO FREE

But you know yourself very well, and are heightened in your awareness of how you stack up to a perfect God. It's pretty easy to become a pagan. Take it from someone who knows.

What changed my perspective? One overwhelming, yet simple revelation:

I am loved by my Father.

There is nothing I can do to make myself not be loved by Him. I wish I had the right words to illuminate the grand scope and beauty of His affections for us. I love how worship leader Cory Asbury explained his song, "Reckless Love."

"When I use the phrase, 'the reckless love of God,' I'm not saying that God Himself is reckless. I am, however, saying that the way He loves, is in many regards, quite so. What I mean is this: He is utterly unconcerned with the consequences of His actions with regards to His own safety, comfort, and well-being. His love isn't crafty or slick. It's not cunning or shrewd. In fact, all things considered, it's quite childlike, and might I even suggest, sometimes downright ridiculous. His love bankrupted heaven for you. His love doesn't consider Himself first. His love isn't selfish or self-serving. He doesn't wonder what He'll gain or lose by putting Himself out there. He simply gives Himself away on the off-chance that one of us might look back at Him and offer ourselves in return.

His love leaves the ninety-nine to find the one every time. To many practical adults, that's a foolish concept. 'But what if He loses the ninety-nine in search of the one?' What if? Finding that one lost sheep is, and will always be, supremely important.

124

His love isn't cautious. No, it's a love that sent His own Son to die a gruesome death on a cross. There's no 'Plan B' with the love of God. He gives His heart so completely, so preposterously, that if refused, most would consider it irreparably broken. Yet He gives Himself away again. The recklessness of His love is seen most clearly in this—it gets Him hurt over and over. Make no mistake, our sin pains His heart. And '70 times 7' is a lot of times to have Your heart broken. Yet He opens up and allows us in every time. His love saw you when you hated Him—when all logic said, 'They'll reject me,' He said, 'I don't care if it kills me. I'm laying My heart on the line.'"[11]

How much does He love? Jesus. Jesus is how much He loves. As my life is more deeply rooted in the love of God (as Paul so eloquently communicated), my focus shifts to the benefits of Christ. I don't say this in the sense that I'm in this for what the Lord can do for me. Ultimately I want *Him* above all that He offers. The beauty of the Father is that when you get Him you get all He offers! What does He make available to me? His spiritual fruit in abundance. Now my spiritual interaction with the Father is not an attempt to stave off His disappointment but rather about a life filled with His love, His peace, His hope, His joy.

My spiritual disciplines, my rhythms, are not so much about how my ministry life is affected or the measure of God's favor on my dealings. The perspective now is "how can I structure my life in order to take on more of God and His kingdom?" We will never have adequate rhythm from a place of fear or insecurity. If we carry an "I better do this so I don't lose ground" mentality we are destined to wander aimlessly and with a parched soul. When I pray, oh what ground is gained! You will never sustain a healthy spiritual or emotional life if it is based in the fear of falling short. It is too cumbersome a load to

11. Cory Asbury, "Cory Asbury," Facebook, accessed May 04, 2018, https://www.facebook.com/coryasburymusic/posts/10158977378510171.

bear. One of Paul's exhortations to the Philippians is fast becoming one of my favorites:

> And now, dear brothers and sisters, one final thing. Fix
> your thoughts on what is true, and honorable, and right,
> and pure, and lovely, and admirable. Think about things
> that are excellent and worthy of praise (Philippians 4:8).

This verse is a glorious starting point in our thought life that will lead to rhythm and a high sensitivity to Holy Spirit! Speaking of fixing our thoughts on what is true and lovely...

CHAPTER 17: SONS, NOT SINNERS

But to all who believed him and accepted him, he gave
the right to become children of God (John 1:12).

I presume you are reading this chapter after walking with me through
all of the preceding chapters. As we arrive at the apex of our journey
through John 1:1-12, hopefully you have sensed a cool, refreshing
undercurrent along the way. This life of faith is not so much about what
we do as it is about what Jesus has done. You and I? We will never do
enough to merit salvation, nor can we do enough to assuage the tension
in our soul. No, we must rely on Him. He does all things well.

I know you are either sitting alone on a couch, holed up in the leather
chair of a somewhat active coffee shop, riding the clouds on an airplane,
or sitting with your toes in the sand on a crowded beach, but humor me
for a moment.

If you have believed Jesus, raise your hand.

If you have accepted Him, raise your hand.

Assuming you just raised your hand, we will proceed with this chapter
with the understanding that it applies directly to you. Regardless of your
grade on the perfection scale, despite your many well-rehearsed faults,
and in light of all your deficiencies. In the next few pages, we are going
to have fun. We have waded through the muck and mire of paradise lost
and the accompanying ignominy, and now we turn the page. We have
tussled with our craving for Babel and elicited the help of Holy Spirit
in removing illegitimate lenses. We have dug in and owned the value of

rhythm. Now we pause and delight. Jesus has accomplished so much on our behalf.

The reason for the prior pages is to bring us to a point of gravity. Unfortunately, it is easy to become so familiar with the life of faith, and more specifically the life of Christendom, that the substance of what Jesus has done does not resonate at the volume it should. We are victims of the fall, but we too, throughout the years of breathing and being, have earned our punishment. We have done enough to justify our death. We have wavered enough. We have chosen poorly enough. We have followed the pull of our flesh with enough frequency that we have no self-reliant claim to the benefits of the cross.

But Jesus.

For those who have believed and accepted, He has given inalienable rights. Yes, those of American citizenship have rights aplenty, but they are paltry in comparison to the beauty bestowed upon those redeemed by the blood of the Lamb.

The kingdom is better.

As my friend Casey Doss says, "Jesus is better."

Let's look more closely at what John is attempting to reveal. There is something revolutionary waiting to be seen. The word "right" is derived from the Greek word *exousia*.[12] If you do a quick scan of the intent behind the word, a new world opens up before you. *Exousia* is attached to several English words:

> *Privilege, force, capacity, competency, freedom, delegated influence, authority, jurisdiction, liberty, power, strength, and right.*

Most translators hone in on the word "right" because it is the most all-encompassing word of the bunch, but the additional English words give texture occasionally lost by repeatedly using only one word.

---

12. James Strong, "Strong's Greek: 1849. ἐξουσία (exousia) -- Power to Act, Authority," accessed May 05, 2018, http://biblehub.com/str/greek/1849.htm.

Let's read John 1:12 again with this new context.

But to *all* who believed him and accepted him, he gave:

Privilege, force, capacity, competency, freedom, delegated influence, authority, jurisdiction, liberty, power, strength—to become children of God.

Recite it until it becomes a well-worn thought pattern in your mind. You are privileged. You have force.

Go ahead and read that a few times. Seriously, read it aloud until it stirs your soul and stirs your spirit. Shout it as a declaration over your life. Recite it until it becomes a well-worn thought pattern in your mind. You are privileged. You have force. You have great capacity to receive and give—in both the spiritual and the natural. You have competency in the life of faith. You have been made free. You have been given influence, authority, and jurisdiction. You are an owner of liberty and a possessor of power and strength. Allow Holy Spirit to settle the meaning deep down into your innermost being. Allow Him a moment to give personal context to every word. Roll each word around in your head and consider its implications and applications. Go ahead and shout a little! Take your time—it feels good.

This textured translation is exciting enough, but there is more weight to be experienced. In the translation for John 1:12 above, the word *children* is used. The New Living Translation, along with a few others, occasionally use a gender-neutral term to signify that a promise or petition is not gender-specific. However, in this instance, doing so diminishes some of our understanding. The more appropriate word is *sons*. *Sons* is derived from the Greek word *huios*.[13] It means what you think it means—a son.

---

13. James Strong, "Strong's Greek: 5207. υἱός (huios) -- a Son," accessed May 05, 2018, http://biblehub.com/greek/5207.htm.

Much dissecting can be done on this terminology, but I will keep it brief. What is startling about the usage is that throughout the Gospels *huios* is used frequently. Specifically, it is the word used to communicate Jesus as *the Son*. It is the same word used to declare Jesus as the Son of God (or Son of Man), and here it is applied to us as "sons of God" when we accept and believe.

Before you panic theologically and call for the heresy police, I completely understand that we are not gods, and neither are we divine. We are not equal to our Lord Jesus, but John, who spent this gospel leveraging the divinity of Christ, saw fit to use the same terminology about you as he did about Jesus. John was not calling us divine, but he was trying to establish that Jesus' work on the cross and His subsequent resurrection so grafted us into the family of God that we are considered sons of God, just like Jesus. This is not a matter of boasting. It is a humbling realization: I am that "in"! This is where I stand in my relationship with the Father and the dynamics of His kingdom. Romans 8:29 essentially calls Jesus our Big Brother, proclaiming Him as "the firstborn among many brothers and sisters." We are sons and daughters—and with this adoption comes rights. You have no idea how saved you really are!

> ## We have embraced a form of false humility never intended by Scripture or heaven.

You are not pitiful. For years we have embraced a theology that accidentally minimizes the accomplishments of Jesus by focusing on how pathetic we are as humans. I am in complete agreement about our destitute state without the grace and mercy offered through the person of Jesus. I am increasingly coming to terms with the utter hopelessness of a life without the hope of Christ. However, once I received Jesus as truth and adjusted the trajectory of my life in His direction, I ceased being pitiful and was transitioned into sonship. This is not to say I do not sin. However, I am no longer identified as a sinner. For generations we have coined the phrase "I am a sinner saved by grace" and in allowing this phrase to be etched in our hearts, we have embraced a form of false humility never intended by Scripture or heaven. Was I once a sinner prior to my encounter with Jesus? Unequivocally, yes. Since that day, was it God's desire for me to continue living under the label of "sinner"? Unequivocally, no. I understand what is behind that phrase. We do not want to become haughty or take hold of the inaccurate idea that we have earned our salvation through our own human effort. But the statement "sinner saved by grace" diminishes the power of the cross and the resurrection. It basically infers that Jesus is capable of getting me through the pearly gates into heaven, but He is not sufficient to empower me to live victoriously over sin in this world. I am not a "sinner saved by grace"! I was a wretch who met Jesus and became a new creation, identified no longer as an enemy of God but as a son in His house with His name branded on my heart instead. I *was* a sinner, but now I am *saved* by grace.

For years I was burdened with a version of the gospel that convinced me I was a worm, a filthy old pitiful sinner saved by the skin of my teeth. The thought was simple. I was unworthy. I should be ashamed of myself. I should just keep my head down and be about the Lord's work; I was not deserving of anything. I type today, imploring you to lift your head! You are not a worm. You are a son. You are not unworthy. You are a daughter. You didn't deserve anything, that is true; but now you are an heir. The whole idea of deserving is intriguing to me. In my home, I am the dad. Ultimately I decide what my children "deserve." I decide if they deserve a cookie or a toy. We usurp the role of the Father when we make declarations of our undeserved-ness. He will decide what we deserve!

I pause for a moment before forging ahead to remind you of some of the opening sentiments of this book. We wrestle and strain in our Christian culture to not be entitled in our thinking. It feels like a greater dimension of humility to say, "I am a sinner." However, humility is best found when gaining perspective of what Jesus has done. If you explore the New Testament long enough, you will come to the realization that God does not call us sinners. Can a son sin? This one certainly has proven capable.

131

LET YOUR HEART GO FREE

But my definition, my title, my label, my nickname is not *sinner*. You are not some poor, pathetic person, completely unworthy to look upon the Lord. You are not a filthy, vile dog who only will enter paradise by the skin of your teeth. Nothing in the new covenant communicates you as such. Allow me for a moment to read you the rights connected to your sonship and citizenship in the kingdom of God. It's OK if you celebrate a little while you read.

CHAPTER 18: RIGHTS

've had very few interactions with the police through the years. Aside from a few speeding tickets, I have a clean record. However, I have watched just enough TV to know that when someone is arrested, the authorities read the perpetrator their rights. Can I take some creative license for a few pages? You have been apprehended by the One who has chased you around every corner of your life. His pursuit has been relentless. He is as consistent as the waves of the ocean. He is as unwavering as the ticking hands of time. His loving patience is long, wide, deep, and high—beyond our comprehension. As one called into a place of authority in the life of faith, allow me to read your rights. The following sentiments are not extracted from my own imagination, nor are they penned by the hands of great philosophers or brilliant theologians. The following is Bible—plain and simple. It's what He has to say about you.

You belong to Christ—you are a new person—your old life is gone and a new life has begun. (See 2 Corinthians 5:17.)

You are a chosen people. You are royal priests—a holy nation—God's very own possession. (See 1 Peter 2:9.)

You died to this life and your *real* life is hidden with Christ in God. (See Colossians 3:3.)

You are a child of God through faith. (See Galatians 3:6.)

You are the temple of the Holy Spirit who lives in you. (See 1 Corinthians 3:16.)

You are no longer slaves; you are now friends of Jesus. (See John 15:15.)

LET YOUR HEART GO FREE

You can now come boldly and confidently into God's presence (without shame). (See Ephesians 3:12.)

You are *His* heir together with Christ—you are an heir of God's glory. (See Romans 8:17.)

You *have been* blessed with every spiritual blessing in heavenly realms. (See Ephesians 1:3.)

You are complete through your union with Christ. (See Colossians 2:10.)

You have not been given a spirit of fear and timidity—you have been given a spirit of power, love, and a sound mind. (See 2 Timothy 1:7.)

You are a citizen of heaven. (See Philippians 3:20.)

You have no more condemnation, so come boldly to the throne of your gracious God. There you *will* receive mercy and *will* find grace to help when you need it most. (See Hebrews 4:16.)

God causes everything to work together for the good of those who love Him and are called according to His purpose. (See Romans 8:28.)

You are God's masterpiece—He created you anew in Christ Jesus, so you *can* do the good things He planned for you long ago. (See Ephesians 2:10.)

If the Son has set you free, you are truly free. (See John 8:36.)

You have been called to live in that freedom—you will walk in freedom because you have devoted yourself to His commandments. (See Psalm 119:45.)

In your distress you prayed, and the Lord set you free. (See Psalm 81:7.)

He has reconciled you to Himself through the death of Jesus. He has brought you into His presence. You are holy and blameless as you stand before Him without a single fault. (See Colossians 1:22.)

He will show you the way of life, granting you the joy of His presence. (See Psalm 16:11.)

This kingdom, of which you are a citizen, is not about what you eat or drink but about the righteousness, peace, joy, and Holy Spirit whom He makes available. (See Romans 14:17.)

The Lord gives you strength—He blesses you with peace. (See Psalm 29:11.)

He will grant you peace as you keep your thoughts on Him. (See Isaiah 26:3.)

Come to me when you are weary and carry heavy burdens, and I *will* give you rest. (See Matthew 11:28.)

He has left you a gift—peace of mind and heart. The peace He has given you is a gift the world cannot give (and the world cannot take it away). (See John 14:27.)

No weapon formed against you will prosper. (See Isaiah 54:17.)

You have been given authority over all the power of the Enemy. Submit to God, and when you resist the Devil he will flee. (See James 4:7.)

You have been qualified to be a partaker of the inheritance of the saints. (See Colossians 1:12.)

You have been delivered from the power of darkness and conveyed into the kingdom of the Son. (See Colossians 1:13.)

These signs will follow you: You will cast out demons, speak in new tongues, you will lay hands on the sick and they will recover. (See Mark 16:17-18.)

And my favorite of all of them:

> Can anything ever separate us from Christ's love? Does it mean he no longer loves us if we have trouble or calamity, or are persecuted, or hungry, or destitute, or in danger, or threatened with death? …No, *despite* all these things, *overwhelming victory* is ours through Christ, who loved us. And I *am convinced* that nothing can ever separate us from God's love. Neither death nor life,

neither angels nor demons, neither our fears for today nor our worries about tomorrow—not even the powers of hell can separate us from God's love. No power in the sky above or in the earth below—indeed, nothing in all creation will ever be able to separate us from the love of God that is *revealed* in Christ Jesus our Lord (Romans 8:35,37-39).

> When I begin to meditate on what Jesus has done, how loved I am, and the new nature into which I have been baptized, everything changes.

Those verses barely scratch the surface of how your Father perceives you because of your willingness to embrace His Son. When I begin to meditate on what Jesus has done, how loved I am, and the new nature into which I have been baptized, everything changes. Will I cross thresholds into sin occasionally? Most likely so. Will I have bad days? Probably. Yet gazing at Jesus has done infinitely more for me than staring at my sin and weakness ever could. Friend, you are free! Joy and peace have been made accessible to you! Love is being lavished upon you! You are a citizen of another dimension. You exist in a parallel reality that is more tangible and full of expression than you imagined possible. The statements above were not plucked from some you-can-do-it, self-help encyclopedia. They were the sound of God communicated through the pen of man, longing to pierce your thoughts and settle deep into who you are. They are the sirens of heaven, awakening the world to the totality of Christ's finished work on the cross and through the empty grave.

He said it. I didn't say it. Your pastor didn't conjure it up. Your mom didn't pass down these nice notes of encouragement. Yahweh, Jesus, Holy Spirit—that is who speaks to you and makes declaration about you.

I have already established that I am a dad. I'm not sure in the moment, outside of the reassurance of the Lord, that you can really know if you are a good parent. You do the best you can and believe the Lord fills in the gaps and deficiencies. However, I knew there were some things I could do to help the cause. I decided, prior to the birth of my first child, that we would establish a few simple institutions in our home as parents. One of those consistent practices is speaking precise declarations to, and over, our son and daughter. Nightly I crawl into bed with my kids and carry on this established ritual. We snuggle and giggle and sing. And each night with the breeze from the ceiling fan kissing our skin and the subtle glow of the night light slightly illuminating our faces, we speak. We speak to our Father, our Jesus, and our Holy Spirit, and we speak to one another. I cannot count the number of times I have recited this liturgy to my daughter. "I love you, you're beautiful, you're smart, you're brave, you're talented, you're passionate, you're pure, and so on." We are now so well versed in this script that she has it set to memory. One day, when my daughter was still pretty new to being three years old, my wife randomly asked her a question. It wasn't a calculated, well-thought-out question. It was one of those passing moments when you are trying to engage your child and get them to talk, primarily because they say so many words incorrectly at that age and it is ridiculously cute to listen to them.

Michelle asked her, "When did you get so beautiful?"

Her unrehearsed, unprompted, unscripted, completely authentic and organic response floored us and with it came a rush of life-changing revelation.

"When daddy said I am." (Selah—pause, and calmly think about that!)

At a young age, she got it. If my daddy said I am beautiful, then I am beautiful. In that moment, she prophesied to me, and as you read these words she is prophesying to you as well. When Daddy says it, you are. His Word over you is more important and truthful than anyone else's word about you. I am fully aware at some point in the future that some idiot little boy or some trifling little girl will come along and, with their actions and words, try to convince her she is not beautiful. They will mishandle her, say something mean, poke at a blemish, point out a weakness. In that moment they are attempting to erode what daddy has been saying all along. They are raising up an unfounded contradiction in her soul. My prayer is that she will have so repeatedly heard daddy, and her ear will be so tuned to my voice, that when this inevitable day comes, she will respond with confidence.

"My daddy has lived longer than you. My daddy is smarter than you. My daddy buys his own clothes, while your mom picks out your underwear. My daddy knew of me while I was in my mom's womb. He sang over me before the world saw me. He spoke truth and life over me before the world knew my name. My daddy was there when I was most vulnerable. He was there when I was helpless and utterly dependent. My daddy knows every birthmark. He saw me crawl. He saw me walk. He saw me fall. He has looked at the dimple on my cheek since the day I was born. He knows every talent I have. He knows what I do well. He also knows my weaknesses. He knows about the times I had a bad attitude. He knows about the days I sinned. He knows the moments when I didn't get it right. He was there for my triumphs and my failures. He has been there through it all. And my daddy says I'm beautiful. His opinion is of higher substance. His evaluation of me is weighted with more information and context. He is right. You are wrong."

Do you see it yet, my friend? We live in a world, a corrupt fallen system, which at every turn attempts to erode your ability to receive love and affirmation from your Father. It is a system longing to convince you of the lie that you are not exactly lovable or worthy. All the while, you have a Father who has been there every step of the way, echoing through eternity. What He says over you is of infinitely greater value than what they say about you!

As cliché as it may seem, you are not defined by the incongruent places in your life. You are not identified for the life processes that do not yet quite match your system of belief. Those moments, those systems of operating, those blind spots are not the lens through which you are viewed by God. He chooses a different lens. He prepared the lens before the foundation of the world. That lens is the Son. You are perceived through the blood. The Christ-lens makes you white as snow. It ushers you into righteousness and blamelessness.

I may be abnormal in this, but the realization that I am ridiculously loved and have been immersed into an eternal brotherhood empowers me with confidence, hope, and faith. It buffets me against the tide of sin, enabling me to rise above the temptation. To know I am a son, even on my worst days, inspires me into a realm of pursuit that all my years of attempted earning never accomplished. We have lost sight of the great instigator in this relationship. It is the Lord who does the inviting. It is He who says, "Come." He demonstrated His love for us first. We are commissioned to grow our roots down into *God's* love (see Ephesians 3:17). The revelation of Ephesus is that if we can, on some level, understand and experience the height, depth, width, and length to which we are loved by God, then we will be made complete with the fullness of life and power (see Ephesians 3:18-19). We have tried really, really hard to love God and love our neighbor as ourselves. The struggle is that we are utterly incapable of doing so with any measure of adequacy unless we have first allowed ourselves to sink deeply into the love God has lavished upon us.

> To know I am a son, even on my worst days, inspires me into a realm of pursuit that all my years of attempted earning never accomplished.

Before we can love, we must receive love. Consider John, whose gospel we have focused on throughout this book. Many scholars hold to the belief that John referred to himself throughout his gospel as "the one Jesus loved." John seemed to understand that his true identity was not wrapped up in how much he loved God. Instead he was identified by the profound truth that he was intensely loved by Jesus. It was of the utmost importance to him that everyone know he was loved by our Lord. Yes, we must love Jesus; but until I have taken in the love of God, how do I even know what to do? We take all our cues from the Lord. How foolhardy to believe I know how to love God until I have meditated on the vast expanse of His love for me. Friend, you are loved—immeasurably. If it takes the next year, root yourself deep into this reality. Nothing works properly without this foundational revelation. *I did not say information.* Intellectually, hearing the phrase "God loves you" has a dullness to it. We have become numb to the information. Revelation transcends and permeates our entire existence. We have a substantial knowledge *about* this truth, but it is altogether different to have real knowledge *of* it. Man can teach you that God loves you. Only the Spirit of God can make it living and breathing in your life and heart.

CHAPTER 19: OUR VOCATION

A s we come to the closing pages of our time together, I want to leave you with one final thought. If I could dream anything for your life, it would be Romans 8:38. I long with the deep places of my heart for sons and daughters of God, like Paul, to be convinced they are loved by God with a love that cannot be torn asunder, even by the strength of ten thousand upon ten thousand horses. You, my friend, are loved. You are not loved like an outsider, welcomed in from the rain. You are not loved like a beggar, shown mercy through the sound of coins landing in a cup. You are not loved even like an orphan, lacking full identity. No, you are loved as a full-fledged, DNA-synced son or daughter of the one true Father.

Through the years, there has been an oft-used expression in the church world. It is, "You were created to worship." This statement rings with truth, and I have no desire to refute its validity. I simply would like to curb our thinking into what I believe to be a better direction and a more all-encompassing truth. Michelle and I were married eleven years before we decided to have children. We loved one another deeply, were the closest of friends, and enjoyed our life together. Due to our desire for flexibility, it took us a while to come around to the idea of kids. Eventually our hearts drifted in the direction of parenthood with a longing to express a different version of our love. There was a longing within us to create children and pour ourselves into them. At no point did I think, "Let's have kids so I can have a miniature version of myself running around, telling me how awesome, great, wonderful, big, strong, and amazing I am." I didn't want kids so I could have a more helpless version of me to bolster how I feel about myself. My yearning for parenthood was not about what I would receive but about the beauty of complete and total giving. My desire for children was not centered on what they could give me. My desire for children was centered on a craving to express myself, my love, and my heart into another. I envisioned their development and the role I would play. I considered the joy of being so intrinsically interwoven with another. Don't get me wrong! When my son tells me I'm a good dad or my daughter tells me I'm handsome, I'm on cloud nine. But this was not the driving force behind me becoming a father. Being "created to worship" implies we were born to *do*; the truth is, we were first born simply to *be*.

Being "created to worship" implies we were born to *do*; the truth is, we were first born simply to *be*.

Without a doubt, the Lord loves our worship and craves our adoration. By all means, extravagantly use your language and actions to express love and affection to the One who has earned it all and then some. But I submit to you that the primary vocation of every human being is to be loved. You weren't so much created for worship as you were created for love. We were all born to be loved. Consider this fact: As you read, there are four living beings flying around the throne of God, each with a unique appearance. One has the face of a human, the others an ox, eagle, and lion respectively. Their only function is to perpetually, and for all eternity, soar in the jet stream above the throne of God, crying "Holy! Holy! Holy!" God already made splendid creatures for the purpose of worship. He made you for love. You were carefully designed, uniquely knit together, and beautifully imagined because God wanted a "you" to express Himself to and through. He made you as an outlet for love, a means of expressing Himself found nowhere else in history.

You weren't created for the primary purpose of worshiping God. You were created for the primary purpose of being loved by God. Upon this foundation, everything in one's life is built. If being loved is identified, well-received, and celebrated sufficiently, the whole of one's life will be healthy and abundant. It is in receiving love that the wells of peace, joy, hope, and life gush wildly. To fall short in identifying, receiving, and celebrating being loved is to shake the foundations of life. All the areas of a person's existence are affected and everything becomes laced with insecurity, fear, and angst.

Your development is more tied to your ability to receive love than to give love

I love how the apostle Paul prays in Ephesians:

> When I think of all this, I fall to my knees and pray to the Father, the Creator of everything in heaven and on earth. I pray that from his glorious, unlimited resources he will empower you with inner strength through his Spirit. Then Christ will make his home in your hearts as you *trust* in him. Your roots will grow down into *God's love* and *keep you strong*. And may you have the power to *understand,* as *all* God's people *should*, how wide, how long, how high, and how deep *his love is*. May you experience the love of Christ, though it is too great to understand fully. *Then* you will be made *complete* with *all* the *fullness* of life and power that comes from God (Ephesians 3:14-19, emphasis mine).

Paul clearly diagnoses the root of soul health, spiritual vitality, and heart freedom—experiencing, understanding, receiving, exploring, and trusting in God's love for us. From this root, all things grow well. If you are anything like me, you have spent much of your spiritual life straining and striving to love God more. Yes, Jesus said the greatest commandment was to love God and love our neighbor. However, the epicenter of faith is the cross where love was dramatically lavished upon humanity. Your development is more tied to your ability to receive love than to give love. It is the seed from which everything meaningful sprouts.

LET YOUR HEART GO FREE

Let's rewind for a moment and put this book in perspective.

Chapter 1: Be

"Any doing not derived from being is hard labor that produces fatigue and frustration." Being rooted in love allows us to be and do.

Chapter 2: Dream

"God's dream for you is Himself." When you sufficiently receive His love, this dream becomes enough for us in the depths of our soul.

Chapters 3 and 4: Paradise Lost and Shame

Sin entered and heaped upon us shame, but when you are convinced you are loved, shame has no hold.

Chapter 5: Dark and Light

The greatest deterrent to our patterns of sin is found in looking into the eyes of love embodied through the person of Jesus.

Chapters 6 and 7: Perceive, and History and Geography

To perceive Jesus well and have the illegitimate filters removed begins at the core nature of God. God is love.

Chapters 8 and 9: Witness and Babel

When immersed in the truth of God's love, our attachments to the lesser satisfactions of this life are loosened. We are empowered to love Jesus more than we love this world.

Chapters 10 and 11: Craving and Think Higher

Our day-to-day cravings and thought life become easier to manage when we keep heaven's love at the forefront of our minds.

Chapter 12: Beach Ball

When you are convinced of love, you are not disabled by your less-than-stellar performance. Your soul isn't crushed under the weight of your human frailty.

Chapter 13: Incremental

To understand that we are loved is to embrace that love is patient. Incremental (over the duration of time) spiritual growth is allowed because love is not in a hurry.

Chapters 14, 15, and 16: Time(s) Management, Rhythm, and Pagan Prayers

Duty, obligation, and appeasement are deficient motivators. They may ignite short bursts of enthusiastic effort but they lack the necessary fuel to sustain a lengthy journey. Love, on the other hand, never runs empty.

Chapters 17 and 18: Sons, Not Sinners and Rights

Love enables us to see ourselves well in the light of Jesus' accomplished work. To be loved is to be valuable.

If I were to boil down this book into one very simple thought, it would go something like this:

"You are loved. Once this fact transitions from an informational notch in your Christian belt into deep, stable truth, everything changes for the better."

Of course, we had to journey together so a statement such as this had better context and meaning.

If I could be so elementary, it seems to me the first truth many of us learned as children in church was indeed the greatest truth:

"Jesus loves me, this I know, for the Bible tells me so."

How much does God love you? Jesus is how much.

> From his abundance we have all received one gracious blessing after another. For the law was given through Moses, but God's unfailing *love* and faithfulness came through Jesus Christ. No one has ever seen God. But the unique One, who is himself God, is near to the Father's heart. He has revealed God to us (John 1:16-18, emphasis mine).

LET YOUR HEART GO FREE

For those who need one more balancing statement: Love doesn't let us off the hook of holiness, devotion, passion, or fulfilling our kingdom assignment. Quite the opposite; it holds us accountable to the highest degree and propels us into a richness and effectiveness of faith beyond our wildest imagination.

To be honest, as I type out the last few lines I have a tinge of sorrow in my heart. I have enjoyed my time with you and I pray you have found it beneficial. I will leave you with one last thought:

Jesus has already made your heart free.

Now, *you* have to *let* your heart go free.

ABOUT THE AUTHOR

For nearly two decades, Jeremy Austill has devoted his life to preaching the gospel and creating hospitable environments for people to engage the presence of God. Through the years Jeremy has served in the body of Christ as youth pastor, evangelist, and church planter, in the past, and now serves in the role of District Youth Director for the Tennessee Ministry Network of the Assemblies of God. Although he has functioned in various assignments, his focus and passion has remained consistent—to lead people into a genuine encounter with the life-changing power of Holy Spirit. Jeremy lives with the great hope that, as citizens of heaven, we can bring the culture of God's kingdom into the earth. He has a deep passion to see followers of Jesus walking in all that was made available through the cross and empty grave. His current responsibilities include hosting camps and conferences, leadership development, missions fundraising, and traveling and preaching in conferences and local churches.

All of the above has been a labor of love alongside Michelle, his wife of over nineteen years. They attended the same youth ministry as teenagers and have served the Lord together as partners through the years. They have been blessed with two beautiful, Jesus-loving children and live in Hendersonville, Tennessee.

Jeremy can be contacted at jaustill@tnaog.org.

CPSIA information can be obtained
at www.ICGtesting.com
Printed in the USA
LVHW051114241120
672558LV00004B/360